Shortcut Staples
SHOPPING LIST

Here's a list of basic ingredients to keep on hand for healthy, low-fat cooking.

Produce

Cabbage, preshredded

Lemons

Mixed vegetables, precut

Mushrooms, presliced

Onions

Peppers (green, red)

Potatoes

Salad greens, precut

Squash

Spinach

Tomatoes

Breads

Boboli crusts

French bread

Hamburger buns (reduced calorie)

Italian bread

Pita bread rounds

Refrigerated pizza crust dough

Tortillas, flour (98%-fat-free)

Canned
(reduced-sodium, low-fat)

Beans (black, kidney, pinto, refried)

Beef broth

Chicken broth

Cream of mushroom soup

Olives

Tomato sauce

Tomatoes: diced, stewed, whole

Grains, Pastas, and Rice

Couscous

Pastas: fettuccine, linguine, penne, spaghetti, tortellini,

Polenta

Rice (boil-in-bag, rice blends)

Dairy

Cheddar cheese (reduced-fat), shredded

Feta cheese (reduced-fat)

Mexican cheese (reduced-fat), shredded

Mozzarella cheese, part-skim, shredded

Parmesan cheese

Sour cream (reduced-fat)

Fish, Meats, and Poultry

Beef: deli roast beef, ground round, tenderloin

Chicken breast halves, skinned

Chicken breast strips, precooked

Pork chops

Shrimp, peeled and deveined

Turkey, ground

Turkey sausage

Frozen

Chicken, diced, cooked

Mixed vegetables

Stir-fry vegetables

Oils/Fats

Butter (light)

Cooking sprays

Oils: olive, sesame, vegetable

Condiments

Garlic, minced

Honey

Mayonnaise (light)

Mustard, Dijon

Olive oil vinaigrette (reduced-fat)

Pasta sauce/spaghetti sauce

Salad dressings (reduced-fat)

Salsa

Soy or teriyaki sauce (low-sodium)

Spreadable fruit, preserves

Vinegar, balsamic

Worcestershire sauce (low-sodium)

Seasonings

Cajun seasoning

Chili powder

Chili seasoning mix

Cinnamon

Garlic powder/garlic salt

Garlic-pepper seasoning

Greek seasoning

Italian seasoning

Lemon-herb seasoning

Mexican seasoning

Taco seasoning mix (low-sodium)

Butterscotch Sundaes with
Rum and Pinapple,
page 166

Hot 'n' Hurried Stir-Fry, page 46

Southwestern Chicken Wraps,
page 18

**Black Forest Trifle,
page 169**

Weight Watchers®

Shortcut COOKBOOK

compiled and edited by
Holley C. Johnson, M.S., R.D.

Oxmoor House®

ISBN: 0-8487-2629-4
Printed in the United States of America
First Printing 2003

Be sure to check with your health-care provider before making any changes in your diet.

OXMOOR HOUSE, INC.
Editor-in-Chief: Nancy Fitzpatrick Wyatt
Executive Editor: Katherine M. Eakin
Art Director: Cynthia R. Cooper
Copy Chief: Catherine Ritter Scholl

Weight Watchers® *Shortcut Cookbook*
Editor: Holley C. Johnson, M.S., R.D., L.D.
Editorial Assistant: Dawn Russell
Senior Designer: Jay Parker
Director, Test Kitchens: Elizabeth Tyler Luckett
Assistant Director, Test Kitchens: Julie Christopher
Recipe Editor: Gayle Hays Sadler
Test Kitchens Staff: Kristi Carter, Jennifer Cofield, Nicole Faber,
    Kathleen Royal Phillips, Jan A. Smith, Elise Weis, Kelley Wilton
Senior Photographer: Jim Bathie
Photographer: Brit Huckabay
Senior Photo Stylist: Kay Clarke
Photo Stylist: Ashley J. Wyatt
Publishing Systems Administrator: Rick Tucker
Director, Production and Distribution: Phillip Lee
Production Coordinator: Larry Hunter
Production Assistant: Faye Porter Bonner

Contributors
Copy Editor: Dolores Hydock
Indexer: Mary Ann Laurens
Recipe Development: Jennifer Cofield, Traci Higgins, Nancy Hughes,
    Jean Kressy, Karen Levin
Test Kitchens Interns: Mary Beth Brookby, Traci Higgins

COVER: Mushroom-Smothered Salisbury Steak, page 125

To order additional publications,
call 1-800-633-4910.

For more books to enrich your life, visit
oxmoorhouse.com

Test Kitchen *Shortcuts*

The Weight Watchers® Shortcut Cookbook **is a collection of 141 kitchen-tested quick and easy recipes.** Each recipe reveals cooking secrets, tricks, and shortcuts from a staff with years of cooking experience, many of whom follow the Weight Watchers program to maintain a healthy weight. We hope that these shortcuts, plus shopping, cooking, and meal planning suggestions will encourage you to prepare healthy, delicious meals for yourself and your family with a minimum of time and effort.

- "I keep extra plastic bags on hand when working in the kitchen. They're perfect for crushing crackers or cookies with a rolling pin, marinating meat, drizzling chocolate, and storing individual portions of food like chopped green bell peppers or onions."
--*Anne Cain, Associate Foods Editor*

- "My family's favorite dish is fajitas so I had to find a way to make cutting up bell peppers a snap. By cutting the four sides off each pepper and discarding the membranes and seeds, I am able to have colorful pepper slices in minutes."
--*Kristi Carter, Test Kitchen Staff*

- "I often double a recipe or cook extra ingredients like pasta, rice or vegetables. I never think of food as "leftovers." I see it more as cooking once to eat twice."
--*Julie Christopher, Assistant Test Kitchen Director*

- "I prefer multi-use cooking utensils to save time, energy and clean up. Three of my favorites are kitchen shears, tongs, and a pizza cutter. The shears can be used to chop fresh herbs, cut fat off or debone meat, or crack nuts. Tongs can be used to turn meat, toss a salad, stir-fry, or serve food. With my pizza cutter, I cube bread quickly for croutons or slice brownies into neat squares – as well as slice pizza."
--*Elizabeth Luckett, Test Kitchen Director*

- "Convenience products like low-fat shredded cheese, bottled minced garlic, pre-washed salad greens, and marinated meat save me a ton of time!"
--*Kelley Wilton, Test Kitchen Staff*

Contents

Shortcut Shortcut hortcut

- "I line baking pans, sheets and casserole dishes with foil for easier clean up. When I make brownies, I line my baking pan with foil. After the brownies have cooled, I lift them out of the pan with the foil and use a pizza cutter to slice into neat bars."

--*Jan Smith, Test Kitchen Staff*

- "To quick cook fresh or frozen vegetables, I toss them into boiling pasta water 3 to 5 minutes before the pasta is done. When the pasta is cooked, so are the veggies."
--*Carolyn Land, Assistant Foods Editor*

- "My three year old is ready to eat as soon as we get home. To speed up cooking, I take time to flatten chicken breasts or other cuts of meat to an even thickness between pieces of wax paper or plastic wrap. A rolling pin or meat mallet work fine, but if I'm really in a hurry, I use the heel of my hand."

--*Alyson Haynes, Associate Foods Editor*

- "Basil is my favorite herb and I use it year round to flavor sandwiches, soups, pasta, even pizza. To quickly slice the basil, I stack several leaves, roll tightly, and then cut them with a sharp knife."
--*Kathy Eakin, Executive Editor*

Our Favorite Recipes

We judge the merits of every recipe, and only the best make the cut. These recipes are so outstanding that they've become our personal favorites.

Beef Tenderloin with Mustard-Wine Sauce (page 95). Got a special occasion planned and you're worried about not being able to eat within your *POINTS* range? Then worry no more when you dine on these 5-*POINT* warm medallions of tender beef drenched in a hearty mustard-wine sauce.

Butterscotch Sundaes with Rum and Pineapple (page 166). Dress up everyday vanilla ice cream with butterscotch sauce, pineapple, and crushed biscotti for an irresistible 4-*POINT* treat.

Chewy Chocolate and Peanut Butter Bars (page 174). Better tasting than your favorite chocolate and peanut butter candy bars, and only 3-*POINTS* each, these fudgy, rich chocolate delights are too good to be true.

Cranberry-Orange Pork Scallopine (page 40). Crushed cranberries and oranges impart an explosion of flavor when you bite into one of these 4-*POINT* sweet pork cutlets.

Grilled Chicken Greek Salad (page 12). This 5-*POINT* salad received the highest possible honors in our test kitchen for its authentic Mediterranean flavor. Not only that, but it's made up of last minute convenience items!

Grilled Tuna and Asparagus Salad (page 91). The combination of fresh grilled tuna and tender asparagus stalks mixed with a tangy vinaigrette dressing makes this summer salad a refreshing 5-*POINT* meal.

Warm Cinnamon Swirls (page 175). Refrigerated roll dough, cinnamon-sugar, and a simple icing make these 1-*POINT* gooey, sweet rolls a snap to throw together.

About Our Recipes

The Weight Watchers® Shortcut Cookbook gives you the nutrition facts you need to make your life easier. We've provided the following useful information with every recipe:

- A number calculated through the **POINTS®** Food System (a component of the **POINTS** Weight-Loss System) from Weight Watchers International, Inc.

- Diabetic exchange values for those who use them as a guide for planning meals

- A complete nutrient analysis per serving

POINTS Food System

Every recipe in the book includes a number calculated using the **POINTS** Food System. This system uses a formula based on the calorie, fat, and fiber content of the food. Foods with more calories and fat (like a slice of pepperoni pizza) receive high numbers, while fruits and vegetables receive low numbers. For more information about the Weight Watchers program and a meeting nearest you, call 1-800-651-6000 or go to www.weightwatchers.com on the internet.

Diabetic Exchanges

Exchange values are provided for people who use them for calorie-controlled diets and for people with diabetes. All foods within a certain group contain approximately the same amount of nutrients and calories, so one serving of a food from a food group can be substituted or exchanged for one serving of any other item on the list. The food groups are starch, vegetable, fruit, milk, meat, and fat. The exchange values are based on the *Exchange Lists for Meal Planning* developed by the American Diabetes Association and The American Dietetic Association.

Nutrient Analysis

Each recipe has a complete list of nutrients, including calories, protein, fat, saturated fat, carbohydrate, dietary fiber, cholesterol, iron, sodium, and calcium. Measurements are abbreviated g (grams) and mg (milligrams). Numbers are based on these assumptions:

- Unless otherwise indicated, meat, poultry, and fish refer to skinned, boned, and cooked servings.
- When we give a range for an ingredient (3 to 3½ cups flour, for instance), we calculate using the lesser amount.
- Some alcohol calories evaporate during heating; the analysis reflects that.
- Only the amount of marinade absorbed by the food is used in calculation.
- Garnishes and optional ingredients are not included in an analysis.

Nutritional values used in our calculations either come from The Food Processor, Version 7.5 (ESHA Research) or are provided by food manufacturers.

No Cook Meals

GRILLED CHICKEN GREEK SALAD

photo, page 22

This salad got top honors in our test kitchen. We loved the flavor and richness of this "full fat" dressing in a small quantity. If you prefer, substitute fat-free Italian dressing for the Greek dressing and save 1–**POINT**.

POINTS:
5

exchanges:
1 Vegetable
3 Very Lean Meat
2 Fat

per serving:
Calories 236
Carbohydrate 6.2g
Fat 13.5g (saturated 3.4g)
Fiber 2.2g
Protein 23.8g
Cholesterol 61mg
Sodium 1215mg
Calcium 76mg
Iron 2.0mg

1   (10-ounce) package torn romaine lettuce (about 8 cups)

2   (6-ounce) packages grilled chicken breast strips (such as Louis Rich)

2   large plum tomatoes, chopped

½   cup sliced cucumber

¼   cup chopped pitted kalamata olives or chopped ripe olives

½   cup (2 ounces) reduced-fat crumbled feta cheese

⅓   cup Greek dressing (such as Ken's with feta, black olives, and olive oil)

Freshly ground black pepper

1. Combine all ingredients in a large bowl; toss gently to coat. Serve immediately. Yield: 4 servings (serving size: 3 cups).

Shortcut

Salad Dressing Secret: For quick made-from-scratch flavor, stir a bit of fresh lemon juice into commercial Greek dressing. Use extra dressing in small quantities as a marinade for chicken or vegetables, or toss with pasta for a quick pasta salad.

MIXED GREENS WITH GRILLED CHICKEN AND POPPY SEED DRESSING

You'll be the envy of the table when you pull this salad out of your lunch bag. Pack the chicken, almonds, and dressing separately and assemble the salad when you're ready to eat.

1   (10-ounce) package European lettuce blend (about 8 cups)

2   (6-ounce) packages grilled chicken breast strips

1   cup whole seedless red grapes

½   cup diced celery

2   tablespoons sliced almonds, toasted

½   cup fat-free poppy seed dressing (such as Maple Grove Farms)

1. Combine all ingredients in a large bowl; toss gently. Yield: 4 servings (serving size: 2½ cups).

LOW POINTS:
4

exchanges:
½ Starch
2 Vegetable
3½ Very Lean Meat

per serving:
Calories 228
Carbohydrate 23.5g
Fat 5.1g (saturated 1.3g)
Fiber 3.4g
Protein 23.0g
Cholesterol 56mg
Sodium 901mg
Calcium 118mg
Iron 2.5mg

Shortcut

Shop the Salad Bar: Stop by the salad bar for chopped celery or look in the produce section for packages of celery sticks. It will save time washing, trimming, and chopping whole celery stalks.

CURRIED CHICKEN SALAD

photo, page 23

Curry powder, used frequently in Indian cooking, adds pungent flavor and a hint of yellow color to this basic and versatile chicken salad.

LOW POINTS:

3

exchanges:
2 Very Lean Meat
1 Fat

per serving:
Calories 134
Carbohydrate 3.1g
Fat 6.5g (saturated 1.4g)
Fiber 0.4g
Protein 15.6g
Cholesterol 49mg
Sodium 730mg
Calcium 8mg
Iron 0.8mg

2   (6-ounce) packages grilled chicken strips, chopped

½   cup diced celery

¼   cup low-fat mayonnaise

2   tablespoons fresh lemon juice

1   teaspoon curry powder

⅛   teaspoon coarsely ground black pepper

1. Combine all ingredients in a large bowl; stir well. Place in an airtight container and chill 2 hours. Yield: 5 servings (serving size: ½ cup).

5 Quick Meals: Make one recipe of Curried Chicken Salad. Enjoy it 5 different ways.

MEAL	POINTS
• 1 medium tomato stuffed with ½ cup Curried Chicken Salad	3
• ½ cup Curried Chicken Salad on 2 slices reduced-calorie wheat bread	4
• ½ cup Curried Chicken Salad on lettuce with 1 ounce toasted pita chips	4
• ½ cup Curried Chicken Salad stuffed in 1 whole wheat pita bread round	4
• ½ cup Curried Chicken Salad with 1 cup cantaloupe slices	4

BLACK-EYED PEA SALAD WITH HAM AND CILANTRO

photo, page 24

Too tired after work to make dinner? Prepare this salad before work, and chill it until dinnertime.

1½   cups chopped tomato (about 1 large)

1   (15.5-ounce) can black-eyed peas, rinsed and drained

1   cup 96%-fat-free diced ham

¼   cup fat-free red wine vinaigrette

2   tablespoons chopped fresh cilantro

1   tablespoon chopped green onions

¼   teaspoon coarsely ground black pepper

1. Combine all ingredients in a large bowl; toss gently. Serve immediately, or cover and chill until ready to serve. Yield: 3 servings (serving size: 1 cup).

LOW POINTS:
4

exchanges:
1½ Starch
1½ Very Lean Meat
1 Lean Meat

per serving:
Calories 209
Carbohydrate 24.0g
Fat 4.8g (saturated 0.2g)
Fiber 4.2g
Protein 18.6g
Cholesterol 40mg
Sodium 1124mg
Calcium 25mg
Iron 2.0mg

Shortcut

How to Chop Cilantro: To quickly chop cilantro, keep the bunch together as it comes from the store. Wash thoroughly under cold running water; shake well to dry. Place the bunch on a cutting board. Using a sharp knife, cut off only the amount of cilantro leaves you need for the recipe. Place the remaining bunch of cilantro, stem end first, in a small glass of water. Cover loosely with plastic wrap and refrigerate up to 1 week. This method also works well with parsley.

COBB SALAD PITAS

Traditional Cobb Salads are full of ingredients like bacon, cheese, tomato, and turkey, and topped with blue cheese. We've taken these ingredients and stuffed them in a pita for when you are on-the-go.

POINTS:
5

exchanges:
2½ Starch
1 Vegetable
1½ Very Lean Meat

per serving:
Calories 283
Carbohydrate 42.1g
Fat 5.7g (saturated 0.9g)
Fiber 6.6g
Protein 18.6g
Cholesterol 23mg
Sodium 1237mg
Calcium 59mg
Iron 3.6mg

1   (12-ounce) package American-style lettuce blend
6   ounces sliced deli smoked turkey, coarsely chopped
⅓   cup bacon pieces (such as Oscar Mayer Real Bacon Recipe Pieces)
⅓   cup low-fat blue cheese salad dressing (such as Kraft Just 2 Good!)
4   whole wheat pita bread rounds, cut in half crosswise
8   cherry tomatoes, halved
2   chopped green onions

1. Combine first 4 ingredients in a medium bowl; toss well.
2. Carefully fill pita pockets with lettuce mixture. Top with cherry tomatoes and green onions. Yield: 4 servings (serving size: 2 pita halves).

Shortcut

Precooked Bacon: The test kitchen didn't think that the conconvience of precooked bacon was worth the added expense. We determined that for recipes like this throw-together sandwich, it is ideal. So pick up a package on your next trip to the store and give it a try. We'd like to know your opinion.

TURKEY AND SLAW WRAPS

These wraps are perfect for a quick dinner, and any leftovers are great
for lunch the next day.

2	cups preshredded cabbage
1	tablespoon thinly sliced green onions
¼	cup reduced-fat ranch dressing
12	(1-ounce) slices fat-free smoked turkey breast
4	(8-inch) 98%-fat-free flour tortillas

1. Combine first 3 ingredients in a small bowl.

2. Place 3 turkey slices on each tortilla; top turkey with about ½ cup coleslaw mixture. Tightly roll tortillas; wrap in parchment paper, if desired. Cut each wrap in half diagonally. Yield: 4 servings (serving size: 1 wrap).

LOW POINTS:
4

exchanges:
2 Starch
2 Very Lean Meat

per serving:
Calories 209
Carbohydrate 31.6g
Fat 1.7g (saturated 0.2g)
Fiber 1.9g
Protein 16.6g
Cholesterol 30mg
Sodium 1393mg
Calcium 27mg
Iron 2.1mg

Shortcut

Wrap It Up: Wrap the sandwich in parchment or wax paper to hold it together for easier slicing and eating. After eating, just toss the paper—no dishwashing required! Parchment paper is now available in sheets and rolls in most supermarkets.

SOUTHWESTERN CHICKEN WRAPS

photo, page 3

Southwestern Chicken Wraps are the perfect sandwiches to eat immediately or to take to work for a hearty, healthy meal. If you like them spicy, use hot salsa or add a little bit of Tabasco sauce. We liked them paired with baked tortilla chips.

POINTS:
5

exchanges:
2 Starch
3 Very Lean Meat

per serving:
Calories 271
Carbohydrate 33.2g
Fat 5.4g (saturated 1.2g)
Fiber 4.5g
Protein 21.5g
Cholesterol 45mg
Sodium 1100mg
Calcium 64mg
Iron 2.8mg

2   (6-ounce) packages grilled chicken breast strips

½   cup salsa

2½   cups assorted salad greens

½   cup canned pinto beans, rinsed and drained

½   ripe avocado, diced

5   (8-inch) 98%-fat-free flour tortillas

1. Combine chicken and salsa in a large bowl; stir well. Add greens, beans, and avocado; toss gently.

2. Spoon 1 cup chicken mixture down center of each tortilla; roll up tortillas. Wrap each tightly in parchment paper, wax paper, or plastic wrap, serve immediately or chill up to 8 hours. Yield: 5 servings (serving size: 1 wrap).

Shortcut

Simple Supper Solution: Make these sandwiches on a day when everyone has a different schedule. All you'll have to do is leave a note—"Dinner is in the fridge."

prep: 10 minutes   **chill:** 8 hours

BEEF AND CHEESE ROLLUPS

These rollups can be made the night before and packed in a lunch bag for school or work.
Cucumber slices and red onions make great fillers, too.

1   (6.5-ounce) container lite spreadable garlic and herb-
      flavored cheese (such as Alouette Lite Garlic and Herb)

4   (8-inch) 98%-fat-free flour tortillas

8   curly leaf lettuce leaves

¾   pound thinly sliced deli roast beef

1. Spread flavored cheese evenly over 1 side of each tortilla; top
each with lettuce and roast beef, leaving a ½-inch border around
edges.

2. Roll up tortillas tightly. Cut in half and serve immediately, or
wrap in plastic wrap and chill up to 8 hours. Yield: 4 servings
(serving size: 1 rollup).

Shortcut

Avoid the Deli Delay: Stop by the deli and order the
sliced roast beef as soon as you enter the supermarket. It
will be ready for pickup when you've finished the rest of
your shopping. List the meat at the beginning and end of
your shopping list so you don't forget to pick it up before
checking out.

POINTS:
7

exchanges:
2 Starch
3½ Very Lean Meat
1 Fat

per serving:
Calories 320
Carbohydrate 27.7g
Fat 11.2g (saturated 7.1g)
Fiber 2.3g
Protein 25.3g
Cholesterol 81mg
Sodium 1442mg
Calcium 91mg
Iron 3.2mg

SLOPPY BARBECUED PORK AND SLAW SANDWICHES

photo, opposite page

Tangy coleslaw has the starring role in this sandwich.

POINTS:
6

exchanges:
2½ Starch
1 Vegetable
2½ Lean Meat

per serving:
Calories 322
Carbohydrate 48.1g
Fat 8.6g (saturated 1.3g)
Fiber 6.7g
Protein 19.4g
Cholesterol 30mg
Sodium 1338mg
Calcium 85mg
Iron 2.9mg

4 cups preshredded cabbage

¼ cup chopped onion

¼ cup cider vinegar

1 tablespoon vegetable oil

1½ tablespoons spicy hot mustard

1½ tablespoons honey

½ teaspoon bottled minced garlic

½ teaspoon pepper

¼ teaspoon salt

2 cups shredded pork with barbecue sauce (such as Lloyd's)

4 (1.4–ounce) light hamburger buns

1. Combine first 9 ingredients in a medium bowl, stirring well.

2. Place shredded pork barbecue in a microwave-safe bowl, and microwave at HIGH 3 minutes or until thoroughly heated. Spoon ½ cup meat mixture onto bottom half of each bun. Spoon coleslaw mixture over meat mixture, using a slotted spoon. Top with remaining bun halves. Yield: 4 servings (serving size: 1 sandwich).

Shortcut

Multi-Tasking: Multi-tasking saves time and is key to shortcut cooking. In this recipe, the barbecue heats in the microwave while you prepare the slaw.

Sloppy Barbecued Pork and Slaw Sandwiches, opposite page

Grilled Chicken Greek Salad,
page 12

Curried Chicken Salad,
page 14

**Black-Eyed Pea Salad
with Ham and Cilantro,
page 15**

No Mess Dinners

ROASTED BELL PEPPER AND MUSHROOM PIZZA

Savor the flavor of many cheeses by using a preshredded light Mexican cheese blend. Chicken and Black Bean Pizza (page 107) and Scrambled Egg Burritos (page 114) use this same cheese blend.

POINTS:
6

exchanges:
2 Starch
2 Vegetable
2 Lean Meat

per serving:
Calories 278
Carbohydrate 36.7g
Fat 7.8g (saturated 3.5g)
Fiber 2.2g
Protein 15.9g
Cholesterol 8mg
Sodium 746mg
Calcium 380mg
Iron 2.7mg

1   (10-ounce) Italian cheese-flavored thin pizza crust
    (such as Boboli)

1   cup tomato and basil pasta sauce

1   (8-ounce) package presliced mushrooms

½   cup bottled roasted red bell peppers, thinly sliced

¾   cup (3 ounces) shredded light Mexican cheese blend
    (such as Sargento)

1. Preheat oven to 450°.

2. Place pizza crust on a 12-inch pizza pan. Spread sauce over pizza crust, leaving a ½-inch border; top with mushrooms and roasted red bell peppers. Sprinkle with cheese. Bake at 450° for 13 to 15 minutes or until cheese melts. Cut into 8 slices before serving. Yield: 4 servings (serving size: 2 slices).

Shortcut

Fresh Mushroom Substitution: Although we prefer the flavor and convenience of fresh mushrooms in this recipe, sliced bottled mushrooms work fine, too. A 4.5-ounce jar should be enough for this recipe.

prep: 3 minutes **cook:** 11 minutes

CHEESE RAVIOLI IN PESTO-TOMATO BROTH

Pair this soup with some fresh fruit and you have a delicious lunch or light supper.
Try substituting refrigerated reduced-fat cheese tortellini for the ravioli.

2   (14-ounce) cans fat-free, less-sodium chicken broth

1   (9-ounce) package refrigerated reduced-fat cheese ravioli

1   (14.5-ounce) can no-salt-added diced tomatoes,
    undrained

¼   cup commercial pesto

2   cups yellow squash, cubed (about 2 medium)

¼   teaspoon salt

¼   teaspoon pepper

1. Bring broth to a boil in a large saucepan. Add ravioli and remaining ingredients; reduce heat, and simmer 8 minutes. Yield: 4 servings (serving size: 1½ cups).

POINTS:
6

exchanges:
2 Starch
1 Vegetable
2 Lean Meat

per serving:
Calories 284
Carbohydrate 35.9g
Fat 10.2g (saturated 3.4g)
Fiber 4.8g
Protein 14.2g
Cholesterol 30mg
Sodium 852mg
Calcium 213mg
Iron 2.2mg

Shortcut

Purchase Extra Pasta: Stock up on packages of refrigerated pasta when they're on sale at a reduced price. Refrigerated pasta can be frozen for up to 3 months. It's the basis for quick meals like this soup and other recipes in this book, including Spinach and Mushroom Alfredo (page 116) and Fettuccini Alfredo with Ham and Peas (page 65).

VEGGIE FRITTATA

This Italian-style omelet features flavored feta cheese and a variety of vegetables.

POINTS:
5

exchanges:
1 Starch
1 Vegetable
1 Lean Meat
1 Medium-Fat Meat

per serving:
Calories 220
Carbohydrate 19.6g
Fat 7.7g (saturated 2.6g)
Fiber 2.6g
Protein 18.7g
Cholesterol 112mg
Sodium 768mg
Calcium 112mg
Iron 4.1mg

Cooking spray

2   cups frozen hash brown potatoes with onions and peppers (such as Ore-Ida Potatoes O'Brien)

1½ cups presliced mushrooms

¾   teaspoon salt

¼   teaspoon freshly ground black pepper

2   cups fresh baby spinach

2   large eggs

1½ cups egg substitute

¼   cup (1 ounce) crumbled feta cheese with basil and sun-dried tomatoes

1. Preheat broiler.

2. Heat a large ovenproof nonstick skillet coated with cooking spray over medium-high heat. Add hash browns; cook, stirring frequently, 7 minutes. Add mushrooms; cook 3 minutes or until mushrooms are tender and hash browns are browned. Sprinkle with salt and pepper. Add spinach; cook 2 minutes or until spinach wilts.

3. Combine eggs and egg substitute in a small bowl; whisk until blended.

4. Reduce heat to medium. Add egg mixture to pan; stir gently. Cook 2 to 3 minutes or until egg mixture is nearly set. Sprinkle with cheese. Place pan in oven; broil 3 minutes or until cheese melts. Slide frittata gently onto a platter, and cut into 4 wedges. Yield: 4 servings (serving size: 1 wedge).

Shortcut

Ovenproof the Skillet: If you're not sure your skillet is oven-proof, wrap the handle with foil before placing it in the oven. The foil protects the handle from the broiler's intense heat.

prep: 9 minutes   **cook:** 11 minutes

ITALIAN-STYLE EGGPLANT
photo, page 42

Serve this dish with a simple green salad for a light meal. If you want something more hearty, serve with ½ cup hot cooked spaghetti for a 7-**POINT** meal.

1   large eggplant

1   large egg, lightly beaten

1   tablespoon water

⅔   cup Italian-seasoned breadcrumbs

¼   teaspoon freshly ground black pepper

Cooking spray

1   cup pizza sauce

1½ cups (6 ounces) preshredded part-skim mozzarella cheese

POINTS:
5

exchanges:
1½ Starch
1 Vegetable
1½ Medium-Fat Meat

per serving:
Calories 265
Carbohydrate 29.7g
Fat 8.8g (saturated 4.9g)
Fiber 5.3g
Protein 17.1g
Cholesterol 78mg
Sodium 1082mg
Calcium 330mg
Iron 1.7mg

1. Preheat broiler.

2. Cut eggplant into 8 (½-inch-thick) slices.

3. Combine egg and water in a shallow bowl. Combine breadcrumbs and pepper in another shallow bowl. Dip eggplant slices in egg mixture, coating both sides; dip in breadcrumbs, turning to coat both sides.

4. Line a baking sheet with foil; coat with cooking spray. Place eggplant on baking sheet; broil 5 to 6 minutes on each side or until eggplant is golden brown and tender. Spoon pizza sauce evenly over eggplant; top evenly with cheese. Return to broiler and broil 1 to 2 minutes or until cheese melts. Yield: 4 servings (serving size: 2 eggplant slices).

Shortcut

Easy Clean Up: Avoid the chore of scrubbing pizza sauce and melted cheese off your baking sheet. Line it with foil for simple clean up.

PROVENÇAL FLOUNDER

photo, page 43

Tomatoes, onions, olives, and basil play prominent roles in this traditional French dish. The bold flavor combination complements the mild flavor of the fish. Serve with crusty French bread to complete the meal.

POINTS:
6

exchanges:
2 Vegetable
3½ Very Lean Meat
2 Fat

per serving:
Calories 265
Carbohydrate 11.1g
Fat 9.8g (saturated 1.8g)
Fiber 2.6g
Protein 33.5g
Cholesterol 82mg
Sodium 742mg
Calcium 67mg
Iron 1.9mg

4	(6-ounce) flounder fillets
½	teaspoon salt
½	teaspoon pepper
1½	cups thinly sliced onion (about 1 medium)
2	cups chopped tomato (about 2 medium)
8	marinated artichoke heart quarters, drained and coarsely chopped
½	cup chopped pitted kalamata olives (about 20) or chopped ripe olives
¼	cup chopped fresh basil

1. Preheat oven to 450°.

2. Cut 4 (12 x 20-inch) rectangles of quick-release foil; fold each rectangle in half; open each.

3. Place 1 fillet on each foil sheet near the fold. Sprinkle fish evenly with salt and pepper. Layer onion and remaining ingredients evenly over fish. Fold edges over to seal securely. Place packets on a baking sheet. Bake at 450° for 10 minutes or until packets are puffed. Remove and let stand 2 minutes. Carefully open packets and transfer contents to 4 individual serving plates. Yield: 4 servings (serving size: 1 packet).

Shortcut

Hassle-Free Foil Packets: Baking the flounder and vegetables in individual foil packets makes cleaning up simple. Toss out the foil and you're finished!

LEMON CRUSTED GROUPER

The buttery rich breadcrumb topping and the lemon sauce are the perfect flavor combinations
for these grouper fillets. This topping is also delicious on red snapper,
orange roughy, or sea bass.

2	tablespoons light mayonnaise
¼	teaspoon grated lemon rind
⅛	teaspoon salt
⅛	teaspoon coarsely ground black pepper
2	(6-ounce) grouper fillets
Cooking spray	
1	teaspoon light butter
⅓	cup dry breadcrumbs
2	lemon wedges

POINTS:
6

exchanges:
1 Starch
4½ Very Lean Meat
1 Fat

per serving:
Calories 288
Carbohydrate 15.3g
Fat 8.2g (saturated 2.0g)
Fiber 0.9g
Protein 36.1g
Cholesterol 72mg
Sodium 608mg
Calcium 68mg
Iron 2.2mg

1. Preheat oven to 450°.

2. Combine first 4 ingredients in a small bowl. Arrange grouper
on a foil-lined broiler pan coated with cooking spray. Spread
mayonnaise mixture evenly over fish.

3. Microwave butter at HIGH until melted; toss with breadcrumbs. Sprinkle crumbs evenly over fish (will not completely
cover). Bake at 450° for 10 minutes or until fish flakes easily when
tested with a fork. Serve with lemon wedges. Yield: 2 servings
(serving size: 1 fillet).

Shortcut

A "Grate" Tip: Grated lemon, lime, or orange rind is a
quick and easy way to add extra flavor to most fish and
shellfish, chicken, and even rice. For extra convenience,
choose a time to grate multiple lemons and store the rind in
a zip-top bag in the freezer. Then, whenever you need it in
a recipe, all you have to do is open the freezer. Use a small
hand-held grater or microplane.

GRILLED HALIBUT WITH OLIVE SALSA

We preferred the briny flavor of the kalamata olives in this salsa, but you can substitute a 2.25-ounce can of chopped ripe olives.

POINTS:
5

exchanges:
5 Very Lean Meat
1 Fat

per serving:
Calories 221
Carbohydrate 2.5g
Fat 6.8g (saturated 0.9g)
Fiber 1.0g
Protein 35.9g
Cholesterol 54mg
Sodium 585mg
Calcium 105mg
Iron 2.4mg

4   (6-ounce) skinless halibut fillets

½   teaspoon salt

¼   teaspoon black pepper

Olive oil-flavored cooking spray

½   cup chopped pitted kalamata olives or chopped ripe olives

2   tablespoons chopped drained oil-packed sun-dried tomato halves

2   tablespoons chopped fresh parsley

½   teaspoon bottled minced garlic

1. Heat a nonstick grill pan over medium-high heat until hot and a drop of water sizzles when dropped on the pan.

2. Sprinkle fish evenly with salt and pepper; coat with cooking spray. Grill 4 to 5 minutes on each side or until fish flakes easily when tested with a fork.

3. While fish cooks, combine olives and remaining ingredients in a small bowl. Serve salsa over fish. Yield: 4 servings (serving size: 1 fillet and 3 tablespoons salsa).

Shortcut

Watch for the Sizzle: It's very important to let the grill pan get hot before cooking the fish. The quickest and safest way to check the temperature is with a drop of water. If the water sizzles, the pan is the correct temperature. You'll get the desired golden to dark brown grill marks without overcooking the fish.

prep: 5 minutes **cook:** 7 minutes **stand:** 3 minutes

DILLED SALMON WITH COUSCOUS AND PEAS

Enjoy this succulent salmon with a glass of Pinot Noir and double the benefits to your heart. Both the omega-3 fat in the fish and the resveratrol in the wine may reduce the risk of heart disease.

Cooking spray

1   teaspoon dried dill, divided

½   teaspoon salt, divided

4   (6-ounce) skinless salmon fillets

1   (14-ounce) can fat-free, less-sodium chicken broth

1   cup frozen green peas

1   cup uncooked couscous

4   lemon wedges

1. Heat a large nonstick skillet coated with cooking spray over medium-high heat.

2. Sprinkle ½ teaspoon dill and ¼ teaspoon salt evenly over salmon and place in skillet. Cook 2 to 3 minutes on each side, or until fish flakes easily when tested with a fork. Transfer salmon to a plate; set aside and keep warm.

3. Add broth to skillet and bring to a boil. Add peas, couscous, remaining ½ teaspoon dill, and ¼ teaspoon salt; stir well. Cover, and remove from heat; let stand 3 to 5 minutes or until liquid is absorbed. Spoon couscous mixture evenly onto serving plates; top with salmon. Serve with lemon wedges. Yield: 4 servings (serving size: 1 fillet and ¾ cup couscous).

POINTS:
7

exchanges:
2 Starch
4½ Very Lean Meat

per serving:
Calories 339
Carbohydrate 27.6g
Fat 6.2g (saturated 1.0g)
Fiber 3.2g
Protein 40.8g
Cholesterol 88mg
Sodium 713mg
Calcium 42mg
Iron 2.3mg

Shortcut

Skillet Savvy: You'll only have one skillet to clean when you prepare this meal.

PAELLA

Paella is Spain's one-dish meal. Saffron rice and a variety of vegetables and meat give this dish its signature flavor. The traditional recipe usually takes 1½ hours to prepare. We've shortened the cook time without sacrificing flavor.

POINTS:
5

exchanges:
2 Starch
1 Vegetable
2 Very Lean Meat

per serving:
Calories 245
Carbohydrate 39.2g
Fat 3.8g (saturated 1.9g)
Fiber 1.9g
Protein 13.3g
Cholesterol 81mg
Sodium 1008mg
Calcium 71mg
Iron 3.0mg

3   cups water

1   (10-ounce) package long-grain saffron rice

2   tablespoons light butter

1   cup frozen chopped green bell pepper

8   ounces peeled and deveined medium shrimp

1   (4-ounce) link andouille chicken sausage, sliced (such as Gerhard's)

½   cup frozen green peas

⅛   teaspoon ground red pepper

1. Combine water, rice, and butter in a large microwave-safe bowl. Cover. Microwave at HIGH 13 minutes. Stir in bell pepper. Cover. Microwave 7 minutes or until rice is tender. Stir in shrimp and remaining ingredients. Microwave 2 minutes or until thoroughly heated. Yield: 6 servings (serving size: about 1 cup).

Shortcut

Micro Meal: Amazing! This entire home-cooked meal is prepared in one bowl in the microwave. Buy peeled and deveined shrimp and use frozen green bell pepper and green peas to cut the prep time considerably.

GRILLED LAMB CHOPS WITH BALSAMIC VEGETABLES

Coat 4 slices of crusty bread with cooking spray and toss on the grill during the last few minutes of cooking. In less than 20 minutes, you'll have a complete meal on the table!

¼   cup fat-free balsamic vinaigrette (such as Girard's)

8   (5-ounce) lean loin lamb chops

4   yellow squash, cut in half lengthwise and sliced

1   red bell pepper, cut into thin strips

1   small red onion, thinly sliced

¼   teaspoon freshly ground black pepper

1. Prepare grill.

2. Brush dressing lightly over both sides of lamb chops.

3. Place vegetables on a large piece of heavy-duty foil; drizzle with remaining dressing and sprinkle with pepper. Bring up sides of foil and fold together to seal, making a packet.

4. Place lamb chops and vegetable packet on grill rack. Cover and grill chops 4 to 6 minutes on each side or until desired degree of doneness (do not turn vegetable packet). Yield: 4 servings (serving size: 2 lamb chops and about 1 cup vegetables).

POINTS:
6

exchanges:
2½ Vegetable
4 Lean Meat

per serving:
Calories 278
Carbohydrate 13.1g
Fat 9.5g (saturated 3.3g)
Fiber 3.5g
Protein 34.8g
Cholesterol 101mg
Sodium 311mg
Calcium 56mg
Iron 4.0mg

Shortcut

Make Ahead Veggie Packets: You can prepare the vegetable packet before you leave for work and refrigerate during the day. Just remember to drizzle vegetables with dressing and sprinkle with pepper before placing packet on the grill. Look for premade foil grill packets at your local supermarket.

prep: 6 minutes   **cook:** 34 minutes

DIRTY RICE WITH KIELBASA AND GREENS

Boxed rice mix and sausage contribute a significant amount of sodium to this dish. If you are watching your sodium intake, substitute fresh baked chicken breast for the sausage.

POINTS:
5

exchanges:
3 Starch
1 Vegetable
1½ Very Lean Meat

per serving:
Calories 279
Carbohydrate 54.1g
Fat 1.5g (saturated 0.5g)
Fiber 1.9g
Protein 12.0g
Cholesterol 16mg
Sodium 1450mg
Calcium 150mg
Iron 2.8mg

Cooking spray

6½ ounces low-fat polska kielbasa, thinly sliced (about 1 cup) (such as Healthy Choice)

⅔ cup frozen chopped onion

½ cup chopped celery

3 cups water

1 (8-ounce) package New Orleans-style dirty rice mix (such as Zatarain's)

1 cup frozen chopped collard greens

1. Heat a large nonstick skillet coated with cooking spray over medium-high heat. Add kielbasa, onion, and celery; cook 5 minutes. Add water and remaining ingredients; stir well. Bring to a boil. Cover, reduce heat, and simmer 25 minutes or until rice is tender and liquid is nearly absorbed. Yield: 4 servings (serving size: 1¾ cups).

Shortcut

Rice Mix Fix: Jump start your recipe by beginning with a flavored rice mix. The rice already has the essential herbs and spices, so all you have to do is add the meat and vegetables.

SANTA FE PORK SUPPER

The spicy flavors of this Southwestern-style meal satisfy both your desire for simplicity and your hearty appetite.

1   (1-pound) pork tenderloin, trimmed

1   tablespoon 40%-less-salt taco seasoning, divided

Cooking spray

1½ cups frozen whole-kernel corn

1   (15-ounce) can black beans, rinsed and drained

½   cup salsa

2   tablespoons water

¼   cup chopped green onions (about 2 small)

POINTS:
6

exchanges:
2 Starch
4 Very Lean Meat

per serving:
Calories 302
Carbohydrate 33.7g
Fat 4.8g (saturated 1.5g)
Fiber 8.4g
Protein 32.6g
Cholesterol 73mg
Sodium 410mg
Calcium 38mg
Iron 3.5mg

1. Cut pork crosswise into 8 pieces. Place between 2 sheets of heavy-duty plastic wrap, and flatten each slice to ¾-inch thickness, using heel of hand, a meat mallet, or a rolling pin. Sprinkle pork with 2 teaspoons taco seasoning; set aside.

2. Place a large nonstick skillet coated with cooking spray over medium-high heat. Add pork; cook 4 minutes on each side.

3. Move pork to one side of pan, stacking pieces, if necessary. Add corn, beans, salsa, water, and remaining taco seasoning to pan; cook 3 minutes or until hot, stirring occasionally. Combine pork and vegetable mixture and cook 3 minutes or until pork is no longer pink. Top with green onions. Yield: 4 servings (serving size: 2 medallions and ½ cup bean mixture).

Shortcut

Knife Know-How: Use a sharp knife when slicing the pork tenderloin into medallions to save time and prevent injury. Sharp knives assure a quick, precise cut.

PORK WITH TUSCAN BEANS

Italian-seasoned tomatoes and olives provide this simple recipe with enormous flavor.
Serve with a crusty piece of bread to capture the essence of this hearty dish.

POINTS:
5

exchanges:
1 Starch
1 Vegetable
3½ Very Lean Meat

per serving:
Calories 249
Carbohydrate 24.0g
Fat 6.5g (saturated 1.7g)
Fiber 7.0g
Protein 26.1g
Cholesterol 53mg
Sodium 1243mg
Calcium 97mg
Iron 3.6mg

1   (1-pound) lemon pepper-marinated pork tenderloin

Olive oil-flavored cooking spray

1   (15.8-ounce) can Great Northern beans, rinsed and
     drained

1   (14.5-ounce) can Italian-style stewed tomatoes, undrained

½   cup chopped pitted kalamata olives or chopped ripe olives

2   tablespoons water

1   teaspoon dried rosemary

1. Remove tenderloin from package, discarding marinade. Slice
pork diagonally across grain into ½-inch-thick slices. Heat a
large nonstick skillet coated with cooking spray over medium-
high heat. Add half of pork, and cook 3 to 4 minutes on each
side or until browned. Remove pork; keep warm. Repeat procedure with remaining pork.

2. Return pork to pan. Add beans and remaining ingredients to
pan. Bring to a boil; cook, stirring constantly, 2 minutes or until
thoroughly heated. Yield: 4 servings (serving size: 3 ounces pork
tenderloin and ¾ cup bean mixture).

Shortcut

Quick Rinse: Before beginning the recipe, place a colander
in the sink; pour beans directly from can into colander.
Rinse under cold running water; drain well.

SZECHUAN PORK AND VEGETABLES

We loved this simple stir-fry over hot cooked rice. Follow the shortcut below, and you'll always have a quick side dish ready for any meal.

1	(1-pound) pork tenderloin, trimmed
2	teaspoons chili paste with garlic
Cooking spray	
1	(16-ounce) bag fresh mixed vegetables (about 4 cups)
⅓	cup reduced-sodium teriyaki sauce
¼	cup water
1	tablespoon cornstarch

POINTS:
5

exchanges:
3 Vegetable
5 Very Lean Meat

per serving:
Calories 271
Carbohydrate 18.8g
Fat 5.6g (saturated 1.8g)
Fiber 3.3g
Protein 36.1g
Cholesterol 98mg
Sodium 958mg
Calcium 37mg
Iron 3.7mg

1. Cut pork crosswise into ¼-inch-thick slices; cut slices in half. Toss pork with chili-garlic paste.

2. Heat a large nonstick skillet coated with cooking spray over medium-high heat. Add pork; sauté 3 to 4 minutes. Transfer to a plate, and set aside.

3. Add vegetables to pan; cook, stirring occasionally, 5 minutes or just until tender.

4. Combine teriyaki sauce, water, and cornstarch in a small bowl; stir with a whisk.

5. Return pork to pan; add cornstarch mixture. Bring to a boil and cook 1 to 2 minutes or until sauce is thick and pork is no longer pink. Yield: 3 servings (serving size: 1⅓ cups pork mixture).

Shortcut

Ready Rice Whenever you cook rice, cook a little extra. Store in an airtight container for up to one week in the refrigerator.

prep: 2 minutes **cook:** 10 minutes

CRANBERRY-ORANGE PORK SCALLOPINE

photo, opposite page

Steam sugar snap peas while the meat cooks and dinner will be ready in less than 15 minutes. Cranberry-orange crushed fruit can be found in the canned fruit section of your local grocery store.

LOW POINTS:
4

exchanges:
½ Fruit
4 Very Lean Meat

per serving:
Calories 168
Carbohydrate 5.0g
Fat 4.9g (saturated 1.7g)
Fiber 0.3g
Protein 24.6g
Cholesterol 71mg
Sodium 572mg
Calcium 23mg
Iron 1.3mg

¾   teaspoon salt

½   teaspoon freshly ground black pepper

½   teaspoon dried thyme

1   pound breakfast pork cutlets (wafer thin)

Cooking spray

⅔   cup orange juice

½   cup fat-free, less-sodium chicken broth

½   cup cranberry-orange crushed fruit (such as Ocean Spray)

1. Combine salt, pepper, and thyme. Sprinkle evenly over both sides of pork cutlets.

2. Heat a large nonstick skillet coated with cooking spray over medium–high heat. Add half of pork, and cook 2 to 3 minutes on each side or until done. Remove pork to a serving plate; keep warm. Repeat process with remaining pork.

3. Add orange juice and chicken broth to pan. Bring to a boil, reduce heat, and cook 1 minute or until slightly thick, scraping pan to loosen browned bits. Add cranberry-orange crushed fruit, and cook 1 minute or until thoroughly heated. Spoon sauce over pork. Yield: 4 servings (serving size: about 2 cutlets and ⅓ cup sauce).

Shortcut

Quick Cook Cutlets: Breakfast pork cutlets are very thin, don't need to be pounded, and cook quickly. The number of pork cutlets in a package differs from store to store. Freeze any leftovers for another meal.

Cranberry-Orange Pork Scallopine,
opposite page

**Italian-Style Eggplant,
page 29**

Provençal Flounder,
page 30

Spicy Posole,
opposite page

SPICY POSOLE

photo, opposite page

This Mexican soup's signature ingredients are pork and hominy. Look for hominy—corn from which the hull and germ have been removed—near the canned corn in your supermarket.

Cooking spray

1   (¾-pound) pork tenderloin, trimmed and cut into
    ¾-inch pieces

2   tablespoons chipotle chiles in adobo sauce

⅔   cup frozen chopped onion

⅔   cup frozen chopped green bell pepper

⅔   cup presliced carrots

2   (14-ounce) cans reduced-sodium beef broth

1   (16-ounce) can white hominy, drained

Chopped fresh cilantro (optional)

LOW **POINTS:**
4

exchanges:
½ Starch
2 Vegetable
3 Very Lean Meat

per serving:
Calories 211
Carbohydrate 19.2g
Fat 4.5g (saturated 1.1g)
Fiber 4.9g
Protein 21.3g
Cholesterol 55mg
Sodium 788mg
Calcium 24mg
Iron 2.3mg

1. Heat a large saucepan coated with cooking spray over medium-high heat. Add pork; stir-fry until no longer pink, about 2 minutes. Remove from pan; set aside.

2. Add chiles, onion, bell pepper, and carrot to pan; coat vegetables with cooking spray. Sauté vegetables 3 minutes.

3. Add reserved pork, beef broth, and hominy. Bring to a boil; reduce heat, and simmer, uncovered, 10 minutes or until vegetables are tender. Ladle into bowls. Sprinkle with cilantro, if desired. Yield: 4 servings (serving size: 1½ cups).

Shortcut

Cold Cut: Place the tenderloin in the freezer for 10 to 15 minutes until firm but not frozen. It will be easier to slice into small pieces.

prep: 3 minutes   **cook:** 9 minutes

HOT 'N' HURRIED STIR-FRY
photo, page 1

We've taken a basic stir-fry mix and added more flavor and texture by mixing in ramen noodles and topping with chopped peanuts.

POINTS:
6

exchanges:
1½ Starch
2 Vegetable
1 Very Lean Meat
1 High-Fat Meat

per serving:
Calories 311
Carbohydrate 45.2g
Fat 7.8g (saturated 1.0g)
Fiber 4.7g
Protein 16.1g
Cholesterol 19mg
Sodium 1202mg
Calcium 68mg
Iron 2.3mg

2   cups water
1   (3-ounce) package low-fat ramen noodles, uncooked
     and crumbled
Cooking spray
1   (24-ounce) package frozen chicken stir-fry mix
     (such as Contessa)
2   teaspoons sugar
¼   teaspoon crushed red pepper
⅓   cup unsalted peanuts, coarsely chopped

1. Pour water into a large nonstick skillet; bring to a boil. Discard seasoning packet from ramen noodles; add noodles to boiling water. Cook 4 minutes or until noodles are tender; drain. Wipe pan dry with paper towels; coat with cooking spray.

2. Heat pan over medium-high heat. Add stir-fry mix and stir-fry seasoning packet to pan. Stir-fry 3 minutes; add sugar and pepper. Cook 1 minute or until thoroughly heated. Stir in noodles, sprinkle with peanuts, and serve immediately. Yield: 4 servings (serving size: 1 cup).

Shortcut

Simplify Seasoning: Use the seasoning or sauce packets provided with package mixes to save time and decrease the number of ingredients in the recipe. Because these sauces are high in sodium, you may choose to discard the packets and use a commercial low-salt substitute such as lite soy sauce. In this recipe, we discard the seasoning packet from the ramen noodles but use the one in the stir-fry.

SPICY CHICKEN AND RICE

We spiced up traditional chicken and rice with some crushed red pepper. While the rice simmers, toss a side salad and dress it with the same Italian dressing used in this recipe.

Cooking spray

1   pound skinless, boneless chicken thighs, cut into 1-inch pieces

¼   teaspoon crushed red pepper

1¾   cups water

1   (6.09-ounce) rice pilaf mix (such as Near East Original Rice Pilaf Mix)

3   tablespoons light Italian dressing

1. Heat a large nonstick skillet coated with cooking spray over medium-high heat.

2. Add chicken and pepper to pan; sauté 6 minutes or until chicken is done. Transfer to a plate and set aside.

3. Add water to pan; bring to a boil. Stir in rice and seasoning packet. Cover, reduce heat, and simmer 10 minutes.

4. Stir in chicken; cover and cook 10 minutes or until liquid is absorbed and chicken is thoroughly heated.

5. Remove from heat; stir in dressing. Yield: 4 servings (serving size: 1 cup).

POINTS:
6

exchanges:
2 Starch
4 Very Lean Meat

per serving:
Calories 302
Carbohydrate 33.2g
Fat 6.7g (saturated 1.4g)
Fiber 1.1g
Protein 26.7g
Cholesterol 94mg
Sodium 820mg
Calcium 60mg
Iron 1.6mg

Shortcut

Ask the Butcher: When grocery shopping, make your first stop at the meat counter. Ask the butcher to bone and skin the chicken thighs while you finish the rest of your shopping. Just don't forget to pick up your package before you check out!

RISOTTO WITH CHICKEN AND PEAS

You can never have too many vegetables. Throw in extra chopped or frozen vegetables like broccoli florets or sliced mushrooms to complement this creamy main course dish.

POINTS:
6

exchanges:
3 Starch
3 Very Lean Meat

per serving:
Calories 331
Carbohydrate 48.9g
Fat 5.0g (saturated 2.1g)
Fiber 4.6g
Protein 23.2g
Cholesterol 42mg
Sodium 1699mg
Calcium 123mg
Iron 2.9mg

Olive oil-flavored cooking spray

½   cup frozen chopped onion

1   (5.5-ounce) package garden vegetable risotto (such as Buitoni)

2⅔ cups water

1   (6-ounce) package grilled boneless chicken breast strips, chopped

1   cup frozen green peas

3   tablespoons freshly grated Parmesan cheese

Freshly ground black pepper

1. Heat a large saucepan coated with cooking spray over medium heat. Add onion; cook, 3 minutes, stirring occasionally.

2. Stir in risotto mix and water. Bring mixture to a boil; cover, reduce heat, and simmer 15 minutes.

3. Stir in chicken and peas. Cook 5 minutes or until rice is just tender and liquid is nearly absorbed. Remove from heat; stir in Parmesan cheese. Sprinkle with pepper. Yield: 3 servings (serving size: 1 cup).

Shortcut

Easy Frozen Peas: Purchase frozen green peas in bags. This way you only have to measure out the amount of peas needed for the recipe. To quickly thaw frozen peas, place in a colander and rinse under cold running water. Drain.

Middle Eastern Chicken Sausage Skillet

The flavors of the Middle East are unique and rely heavily on the use of herbs and spices. Because eating pork is forbidden in this culture, we used chicken as the meat alternative.

1	(12-ounce) package fully cooked spicy chicken sausage
1¾	cups water
2	cups packaged matchstick-cut carrots
1	teaspoon ground cumin
¼	teaspoon ground cinnamon
1	(5.8-ounce) package garlic-flavored couscous
⅓	cup golden raisins

Plain low-fat yogurt (optional)

1. Cut sausage into ¼-inch slices. Set aside.

2. Combine water, next 3 ingredients, and seasoning packet from couscous in a saucepan; bring to a boil over medium-high heat. Cover; reduce heat, and simmer 3 minutes or until carrots are tender. Stir in couscous, sausage, and golden raisins. Cover, and let stand 5 minutes or until liquid is absorbed. Serve with yogurt, if desired. Yield: 5 servings (serving size: 1 cup).

POINTS:
5

exchanges:
2 Starch
2 Vegetable
1½ Medium-Fat Meat

per serving:
Calories 272
Carbohydrate 41.7g
Fat 7.4g (saturated 2.0g)
Fiber 5.3g
Protein 13.4g
Cholesterol 50mg
Sodium 640mg
Calcium 36mg
Iron 1.7mg

Shortcut

Pick Up Matchsticks: Look for matchstick-cut carrots in the produce section of the supermarket. The days of patiently cutting carrots into little sticks are over!

SAUSAGE WITH APPLES AND SAUERKRAUT

It doesn't have to be Oktoberfest for you to enjoy a robust German-style supper. Save a few extra **POINTS** for the end of the day to enjoy this dish with your favorite German beer.

LOW POINTS:
4

exchanges:
½ Starch
2 Fruit
2 Very Lean Meat

per serving:
Calories 236
Carbohydrate 41.0g
Fat 3.3g (saturated 1.0g)
Fiber 4.6g
Protein 13.7g
Cholesterol 35mg
Sodium 1533mg
Calcium 65mg
Iron 1.8mg

Cooking spray

1   (14-ounce) package turkey smoked sausage (such as Healthy Choice), cut into 3-inch pieces and halved lengthwise

1¾ cups frozen chopped onion

2   large Braeburn apples, sliced and cubed

1   (16-ounce) package refrigerated sauerkraut, drained

2   teaspoons caraway seeds

¼   teaspoon pepper

1. Heat a large nonstick skillet coated with cooking spray over medium-high heat. Add sausage, cut sides down; cook 4 minutes or until browned. Add onion; cook 2 minutes, stirring occasionally. Add apple; cook 6 minutes or until apple and onion are tender. Add sauerkraut and remaining ingredients. Reduce heat to medium; cook 3 minutes or until thoroughly heated, stirring occasionally. Yield: 4 servings (serving size: 1½ cups).

Shortcut

Slice with Ease: An apple corer is a round gadget that looks like a wagon wheel. Use it to quickly core and slice apples into thick wedges. Use a chef's knife to cut the wedges into cubes.

prep: 1 minute   **cook:** 7 minutes

BLUE CHEESE-WALNUT MACARONI AND CHEESE

Blue cheese and walnuts help turn this ordinary macaroni and cheese dish into an extraordinary meal. Toss together a quick salad with spinach and pear slices while the macaroni and cheese bakes.

1   (10-ounce) low-fat macaroni and cheese frozen entrée

2   teaspoons chopped walnuts

2   tablespoons crumbled blue cheese

2   tablespoons dry breadcrumbs

Cooking spray

POINTS:

8

exchanges:

2½ Starch
2 Medium-Fat Meat

1. Preheat broiler.

2. Prepare entrée according to microwave directions.

3. Remove from microwave and stir in walnuts and blue cheese. Sprinkle top with breadcrumbs and coat lightly with cooking spray.

4. Broil 2 to 3 minutes or until crumbs are golden brown. Yield: 1 serving (serving size: 1 entrée).

per serving:

Calories 355
Carbohydrate 45.6g
Fat 11.8g (saturated 5.6g)
Fiber 2.5g
Protein 17.3g
Cholesterol 29mg
Sodium 795mg
Calcium 326mg
Iron 1.0mg

Shortcut

Jump-Start Ingredient: Use a prepared macaroni and cheese entrée to get a jump start on supper. With these easy stir-in ingredients, the entire meal takes only 8 minutes!

prep: 2 minutes **cook:** 10 minutes

VEGETABLE MACARONI AND CHEESE

Just about any 0-**POINT** vegetable can be substituted for the broccoli in this versatile recipe.

POINTS:
7

exchanges:
3 Starch
1 Vegetable
2 Very Lean Meat

per serving:
Calories 311
Carbohydrate 49.9g
Fat 8.2g (saturated 3.9g)
Fiber 4.4g
Protein 16.3g
Cholesterol 22mg
Sodium 628mg
Calcium 305mg
Iron 1.5mg

½   cup small broccoli florets

2   teaspoons water

1   (10-ounce) low-fat macaroni and cheese frozen entrée

2   tablespoons frozen chopped onion

2   teaspoons chopped fresh basil or parsley

½   tomato, sliced

1. Preheat oven to 450°.

2. Place broccoli and water in a small microwave-safe dish; cover with heavy-duty plastic wrap. Microwave at HIGH 1 to 2 minutes or just until tender. Drain well and set aside.

3. Prepare entrée according to microwave directions.

4. Stir in broccoli, onion, and basil. Top with tomato slices.

5. Bake at 450° for 4 minutes or until browned. Yield: 1 serving (serving size: 1 entrée).

Shortcut

Fresh Herbs: We use fresh herbs in many recipes because of their superior flavor. If you prefer the convenience of dried herbs, remember that the flavor is concentrated, so use ⅓ the amount of dried herbs as you would fresh.

POLENTA WITH MUSHROOMS, ZUCCHINI, AND MOZZARELLA

Polenta is a fast alternative to pasta, rice, or mashed potatoes. Encourage your family to give it a try by combining the polenta with more familiar ingredients.

Olive oil-flavored cooking spray

1   (16-ounce) tube of polenta, cut into 8 slices

3   cups diced zucchini (about 2 medium)

1   (8-ounce) package presliced mushrooms

1   (14.5-ounce) can diced tomatoes with basil, garlic, and oregano, drained (such as Hunt's)

1   cup (4 ounces) preshredded part-skim mozzarella cheese

1. Heat a large nonstick skillet coated with cooking spray over medium-high heat. Add polenta rounds and cook 3 minutes on each side or until lightly browned. Remove from pan; set aside and keep warm.

2. Add zucchini and mushrooms to pan; sauté 7 minutes or until tender. Stir in tomatoes, and cook until thoroughly heated.

3. Place 2 polenta rounds on each of 4 serving plates. Spoon vegetable mixture over polenta. Top with cheese. Yield: 4 servings (serving size: 2 polenta rounds, 1 cup vegetable mixture, and ¼ cup cheese).

LOW POINTS:
4

exchanges:
1 Starch
2 Vegetable
1 Medium-Fat Meat

per serving:
Calories 198
Carbohydrate 26.0g
Fat 4.8g (saturated 2.9g)
Fiber 3.6g
Protein 12.0g
Cholesterol 16mg
Sodium 681mg
Calcium 234mg
Iron 2.5mg

Shortcut

Prepared Polenta: You can find refrigerated tubes of polenta in a variety of flavors in the produce section of the grocery store. This delicious product is ready in less than the time it takes to boil water for pasta or rice.

cook: 5 minutes   **stand:** 15 minutes

WHITE BEAN AND ASPARAGUS TABBOULEH

Tabbouleh is a Middle Eastern dish made primarily of bulgur wheat. Using a commercial mix allows you to capture the flavors of traditional tabbouleh with fewer ingredients.

POINTS:

5

exchanges:

2 Starch
1 Vegetable
1 Very Lean Meat
½ Fat

per serving:

Calories 233
Carbohydrate 28.9g
Fat 9.8g (saturated 1.4g)
Fiber 7.8g
Protein 11.0g
Cholesterol 0mg
Sodium 877mg
Calcium 80mg
Iron 2.9mg

1   (5.25-ounce) package tabbouleh mix

1   cup boiling water

1   (10-ounce) package frozen asparagus spears

1   (16-ounce) can navy beans, rinsed and drained

1½ tablespoons fresh lemon juice

1   tablespoon extra-virgin olive oil

¼   teaspoon salt

⅛   teaspoon coarsely ground black pepper

1. Combine tabbouleh mix (bulgur wheat and spice packet) and boiling water in a large bowl. Cover and let stand at room temperature 15 minutes or until water is absorbed.

2. Cook asparagus according to package directions; drain in a colander, and cool under running water. Drain well; cut into bite-sized pieces.

3. Combine tabbouleh mix, asparagus, beans, and remaining ingredients in a large bowl. Yield: 3 servings (serving size: 1⅓ cup).

Shortcut

Dinner Anytime: Keep these non-perishable ingredients on hand so you can come home and pull together a meal in less than 20 minutes. While the tabbouleh stands, prepare a green salad with low-fat dressing for a 6-**POINT** meal.

prep: 3 minutes **cook:** 12 minutes

GRILLED PESTO SALMON
photo, page 61

Surprise guests? No problem. This elegant meal is ready in less than 15 minutes. While the salmon grills, prepare orzo and steamed green beans for an 8-**POINT** meal.

Cooking spray

4   (6-ounce) salmon fillets

¼   teaspoon salt

¼   teaspoon freshly ground black pepper

3   tablespoons refrigerated pesto

3   tablespoons dry white wine

1. Heat a large grill pan coated with cooking spray over medium heat.

2. Sprinkle salmon evenly with salt and pepper. Set aside.

3. Combine pesto and wine, stirring well.

4. Place fillets on grill pan, and grill 6 minutes on each side or until fish flakes easily when tested with a fork. Serve fish with pesto sauce. Yield: 4 servings (serving size: 1 salmon fillet and 1½ tablespoons sauce).

POINTS:

6

exchanges:

5 Very Lean Meat

1 Fat

per serving:

Calories 280

Carbohydrate 1.0g

Fat 11.7g (saturated 2.5g)

Fiber 0.4g

Protein 38.9g

Cholesterol 100mg

Sodium 360mg

Calcium 108mg

Iron 1.9mg

Shortcut

Quick Grill: A grill pan heats quickly and evenly, and, since food is raised up above the bottom of the pan, clean up is easy. Some grill pans are attractive enough to use as serving pieces, so there's one less dish to wash!

FETTUCCINE ALFREDO WITH SALMON AND SUGAR SNAP PEAS

Stir the salmon into the pasta mixture or serve it on top for an elegant presentation. For a sweet after-dinner treat, enjoy Mixed Berries with Raspberry Cream Sauce (page 156).

POINTS:

6

exchanges:

2 Starch
1 Vegetable
2 Very Lean Meat
1 Fat

per serving:

Calories 312
Carbohydrate 41.9g
Fat 7.9g (saturated 3.6g)
Fiber 3.0g
Protein 16.2g
Cholesterol 27mg
Sodium 640mg
Calcium 136mg
Iron 1.1mg

1	(9-ounce) package refrigerated fettuccine
1	(6-ounce) package fresh sugar snap peas, trimmed
1	(10-ounce) container refrigerated light Alfredo sauce
½	cup thinly sliced smoked salmon
1	teaspoon chopped fresh dill
½	teaspoon freshly ground black pepper

1. Cook fettuccine according to package directions, omitting salt and fat; add sugar snap peas during last 1 minute of cooking time. Drain well.

2. Place Alfredo sauce in a large microwave-safe serving bowl; microwave at HIGH 1 minute or until thoroughly heated.

3. Add pasta and peas, salmon, dill, and pepper to Alfredo sauce; toss well. Serve immediately. Yield: 4 servings (serving size: about 1 cup).

Shortcut

No Need to Trim: Trimming sugar snap peas is time consuming. Look for the 6-ounce packages of fresh, trimmed sugar snap peas in the produce section of your supermarket. If you can't find trimmed peas, gather the peas with like ends facing the same direction, and slice off the tips with a chef's knife.

Pot Roast with Balsamic Onions

Your family will never suspect you made dinner at the last minute when they taste this tender roast with sweet onions in a rich balsamic sauce. For dessert, treat them to a Quadruple Chocolate Sundae (page 168), like the one pictured on page 63.

1   (16-ounce) package fully cooked beef pot roast (such as Thomas E. Wilson)

Cooking spray

1   large onion, thinly sliced (about 2 cups)

1   tablespoon light butter

½   teaspoon sugar

1   teaspoon balsamic vinegar

¼   teaspoon salt

¼   teaspoon black pepper

LOW POINTS:
4

exchanges:
1 Vegetable
3 Lean Meat

per serving:
Calories 184
Carbohydrate 8.4g
Fat 5.6g (saturated 2.4g)
Fiber 1.1g
Protein 22.3g
Cholesterol 65mg
Sodium 500mg
Calcium 13mg
Iron 2.6mg

1. Heat beef according to package directions. Remove beef from package, reserving liquid. Let stand 2 minutes. Slice into 8 pieces.
2. Meanwhile, place a large nonstick skillet coated with cooking spray over medium-high heat. Add onion; cook 10 minutes or until browned, stirring constantly. Add reserved liquid, butter, and remaining ingredients; stir well. Bring to a boil. Boil 30 seconds or until thoroughly heated. Serve warm. Yield: 4 servings (serving size: 2 slices pot roast and 2 tablespoons sauce).

Shortcut

Dinner in No Time: Start with a fully cooked beef pot roast now available in most supermarkets, and add a few basic ingredients. While the onions are caramelizing and the roast is heating, prepare frozen mashed potatoes and a tossed salad. You'll have a full meal on the table in less than 20 minutes.

prep: 6 minutes   **cook:** 9 minutes   **stand:** 5 minutes

JAMBALAYA

While the Jambalaya is standing, slice a cucumber and tomato and toss them with fat-free Italian dressing for a quick side dish.

LOW **POINTS:**
4

exchanges:
1½ Starch
2 Vegetable
1½ Very Lean Meat

per serving:
Calories 229
Carbohydrate 35.3g
Fat 3.5g (saturated 0.8g)
Fiber 3.6g
Protein 13.0g
Cholesterol 23mg
Sodium 1074mg
Calcium 24mg
Iron 1.3mg

Cooking spray

¾ cup diced green bell pepper (about 1 medium)

1⅔ cups water

1½ cups uncooked instant brown rice

1 (14.5-ounce) can diced tomatoes with green pepper, celery, and onions (such as Hunt's)

1¼ cups diced reduced-fat ham

1 teaspoon Old Bay seasoning

1. Place a large nonstick skillet coated with cooking spray over medium-high heat. Add green bell pepper; sauté 4 minutes or until lightly browned. Stir in water and remaining ingredients; bring to a boil. Cover, reduce heat, and simmer 5 minutes. Remove from heat and let stand 5 minutes. Yield: 4 servings (serving size: 1 cup).

Shortcut

Use the Weekend: When you're in a hurry, the last thing you want to do is spend time chopping ingredients. What's the solution? On the weekend, when you have a little more time, chop several green peppers and onions. Freeze in a single layer on a baking sheet to avoid having a solid mass of vegetables. Once the vegetables freeze, divide into ½-cup or 1-cup portions in heavy-duty zip-top bags, label, and return to the freezer. Next time a recipe calls for chopped peppers or onions, you'll be prepared.

**Grilled Pesto Salmon,
page 57**

Chicken and Pasta Florentine,
page 69

Quadruple Chocolate Sundae,
page 168

Roasted Rosemary Potatoes,
page 151

FETTUCCINE ALFREDO WITH HAM AND PEAS

This rich, creamy pasta sauce, sweet green peas, and salty ham create a wonderful flavor combination. We suggest serving it with a sourdough roll and fresh fruit for a 9-**POINT** meal.

1	(9-ounce) package refrigerated fettuccine
1	(10-ounce) container refrigerated light Alfredo sauce
1	cup diced reduced-fat ham
1	cup frozen petite green peas
¼	teaspoon freshly ground black pepper

1. Cook fettuccine according to package directions, omitting salt and fat; drain well.

2. Place Alfredo sauce in a large microwave-safe serving bowl; microwave at HIGH 1 minute or until thoroughly heated.

3. Add pasta, ham, peas, and pepper to Alfredo sauce; toss well. Serve immediately. Yield: 4 servings (serving size: 1 cup).

POINTS:
7

exchanges:
3 Starch
2 Lean Meat

per serving:
Calories 353
Carbohydrate 44.1g
Fat 9.2g (saturated 4.1g)
Fiber 3.6g
Protein 21.1g
Cholesterol 41mg
Sodium 966mg
Calcium 126mg
Iron 1.1mg

Shortcut

Fresh Pepper Pizazz: Just because you like to cook quick doesn't mean you have to sacrifice flavor. In the spice sections of the grocery store, pick up a jar of whole black peppercorns with the mill attached. Keep it in easy reach on your kitchen counter. The next time a recipe calls for freshly ground pepper, it's only a twist of the mill away.

prep: 2 minutes   **cook:** 15 minutes

TEX-MEX MACARONI AND CHEESE

Make a fast family meal by dressing up multiple single serving entrées. This plain macaroni and cheese gets a Southwestern flair when sausage and green chiles are added.

POINTS:
6

exchanges:
2 Starch
2½ Lean Meat

per serving:
Calories 291
Carbohydrate 35.6g
Fat 7.2g (saturated 3.2g)
Fiber 2.4g
Protein 17.9g
Cholesterol 38mg
Sodium 813mg
Calcium 223mg
Iron 1.5mg

3   (10-ounce) low-fat macaroni and cheese frozen entrées

Cooking spray

6   ounces 97%-fat-free sausage (such as Jimmy Dean)

½   teaspoon ground cumin

1   (4.5-ounce) can chopped green chiles, drained

⅓   cup frozen chopped onion

1. Preheat oven to 450°.

2. Prepare entrées according to microwave directions.

3. Place a large nonstick skillet coated with cooking spray over medium-high heat. Add sausage; cook until meat is browned, stirring to crumble. Drain well. Combine sausage, cumin, green chiles, and onion.

4. Spoon macaroni and cheese into an 8-inch square baking dish coated with cooking spray. Stir in sausage mixture. Bake at 450° for 6 minutes or until lightly browned and thoroughly heated. Yield: 4 servings (serving size: 1 cup).

Shortcut

Easy Draining Techniques: Heart-healthy recipes that use crumbled sausage or lean ground beef often say to drain the meat after cooking. There are two quick ways to do this. Pat the meat dry in the pan with several paper towels or line a colander with paper towels and pour the meat into it.

prep: 1 minute   **cook:** 11 minutes   **stand:** 3 minutes

CHICKEN PASTA PRIMAVERA

Experience the flavors of spring when you combine fresh vegetables, grilled chicken, and pasta. For a refreshing dessert, serve Honey Walnut Fruit Cup (page 161) or Raspberry-Strawberry Parfaits (page 163).

1   (16-ounce) package fresh vegetable medley (broccoli, cauliflower, and carrot)

1   (14-ounce) can fat-free, less-sodium chicken broth

½   cup water

1   (4.8-ounce) package angel hair pasta with herbs

1   (6-ounce) package refrigerated grilled chicken breast strips, chopped

¼   cup preshredded fresh Parmesan cheese

¼   teaspoon freshly ground black pepper

1. Cook vegetables in microwave according to package directions.

2. While vegetables cook, combine chicken broth and water in a medium saucepan; bring to a boil. Reduce heat; stir in pasta and seasoning packet. Simmer, uncovered, 5 minutes or until pasta is tender, stirring occasionally. Remove from heat, and stir in cooked vegetables and chicken. Cover and let stand 3 minutes. Sprinkle with cheese and pepper. Serve immediately. Yield: 4 servings (serving size: 1¼ cups).

LOW **POINTS:**
4

exchanges:
1½ Starch
2 Vegetable
2½ Very Lean Meat

per serving:
Calories 244
Carbohydrate 32.7g
Fat 4.8g (saturated 1.8g)
Fiber 4.3g
Protein 19.1g
Cholesterol 32mg
Sodium 1186mg
Calcium 128mg
Iron 2.0mg

Shortcut

Ready-To-Go Vegetables: Grocery stores now carry fresh vegetables that are not only ready-to-eat, but are ready to microwave in their original bag. This new packaging not only saves you from washing an extra bowl, it also preserves the water-soluble nutrients.

prep: 9 minutes   **cook:** 3 minutes

ORANGE-CHICKEN COUSCOUS

Couscous is a speedy alternative to rice. This tiny, fluffy pasta has to stand about 5 minutes after it is added to the boiling water.

POINTS:
5

exchanges:
1½ Starch
1 Fruit
2 Very Lean Meat

per serving:
Calories 258
Carbohydrate 39.5g
Fat 4.8g (saturated 1.0g)
Fiber 2.5g
Protein 15.7g
Cholesterol 28mg
Sodium 858mg
Calcium 26mg
Iron 1.6mg

1   (5.6-ounce) package couscous mix with toasted pine nuts (such as Near East)

1   (11-ounce) can mandarin oranges in light syrup

1   (6-ounce) package cooked grilled chicken strips

¾   cup diced zucchini (about 1 small)

2   tablespoons sliced almonds, toasted

¼   teaspoon salt

⅛   teaspoon freshly ground black pepper

1. Prepare couscous according to package directions, omitting fat. Transfer to a large bowl; fluff with a fork; set aside.

2. Drain oranges, reserving ¼ cup syrup. Combine couscous, reserved syrup, chicken, zucchini, almonds, salt, and pepper; toss well. Add oranges, and toss gently. Yield: 4 servings (serving size: 1¼ cups).

Shortcut

Nut Toasting Tips: Toasting brings out the maximum flavor of most nuts. If you want to toast almonds for the couscous, put them in a dry skillet and cook over medium heat for about 5 minutes, stirring often. While you're at it, go ahead and toast extra nuts to keep on hand for other recipes. Label and store in the freezer for up to 6 months. They'll be ready to toss on simple salads and desserts at the last minute.

prep: 6 minutes **cook:** 13 minutes

CHICKEN AND PASTA FLORENTINE

photo, page 62

Once you stir fresh spinach, tomatoes, and chopped cooked chicken into the creamy pasta and cheese, dinner is only minutes away.

2   cups firmly packed baby spinach

3   (10-ounce) low-fat macaroni and cheese frozen entrées

1   cup chopped seeded tomato (about 2 medium)

1   cup chopped cooked chicken breast

¼   teaspoon pepper

Cooking spray

¼   cup grated Parmesan cheese

⅓   cup dry breadcrumbs

1. Preheat broiler.

2. Place spinach in a small microwave-safe bowl; cover with heavy-duty plastic wrap, and microwave at HIGH 1 to 2 minutes or just until spinach wilts. Drain well and set aside.

3. Prepare entrées according to microwave directions.

4. Combine macaroni and cheese, spinach, tomato, chicken, and pepper; stir well. Spoon into an 8-inch square baking dish coated with cooking spray.

5. Combine cheese and breadcrumbs; sprinkle evenly over macaroni and cheese mixture, and coat with cooking spray. Broil 2 to 3 minutes or until crumbs are golden brown. Yield: 4 servings (serving size: 1¼ cups).

POINTS:
7

exchanges:
2½ Starch
1 Vegetable
3 Very Lean Meat

per serving:
Calories 341
Carbohydrate 42.4g
Fat 8.6g (saturated 4.2g)
Fiber 3.0g
Protein 24.0g
Cholesterol 40mg
Sodium 957mg
Calcium 322mg
Iron 1.6mg

Shortcut

Choose Your Favorite Chicken: When you see chopped cooked chicken on an ingredient list, don't take the extra time to prepare fresh chicken use leftovers, meat pulled off a deli-roasted chicken, refrigerated cooked chicken, or just thawed frozen cooked chicken chunks.

CHICKEN PESTO POCKETS

Don't be intimidated by the time it takes to bake this recipe. Use that time to prepare a salad or side dish or just to relax. You'll be so pleased you waited when you cut into one of these crispy, juicy chicken breasts oozing with creamy pesto.

POINTS:
6

exchanges:
½ Starch
4½ Very Lean Meat
1 Fat

per serving:
Calories 258
Carbohydrate 7.4g
Fat 9.8g (saturated 4.6g)
Fiber 0.6g
Protein 32.5g
Cholesterol 82mg
Sodium 516mg
Calcium 165mg
Iron 1.4mg

⅓ cup light cream cheese

¼ cup (1 ounce) shredded Parmesan cheese

2 tablespoons refrigerated pesto

¼ cup Italian-seasoned breadcrumbs

¼ teaspoon freshly ground black pepper

4 (4-ounce) skinless, boneless chicken breast halves

Cooking spray

1. Preheat oven to 400°.

2. Combine first 3 ingredients in a small bowl; set aside.

3. Combine breadcrumbs and pepper in a shallow dish; set aside.

4. Cut a horizontal slit through thickest portion of each chicken breast half to form a pocket; divide pesto mixture evenly among pockets. Dredge chicken in breadcrumb mixture.

5. Place chicken breasts on a foil-lined baking sheet coated with cooking spray. Coat chicken lightly with cooking spray. Bake at 400° for 20 to 22 minutes or until chicken is done. Remove from oven, and let stand 3 to 4 minutes before serving. Yield: 4 servings (serving size: 1 chicken breast half).

Shortcut

Pre-Meal Preparation: If you won't have much time in the evening to prepare dinner, cut, stuff, and refrigerate the chicken breasts the night before or early that day. When you're ready to eat, bread the stuffed breasts and bake.

prep: 3 minutes   **cook:** 17 minutes

GREEK CHICKEN

Experience the wonders of Mediterranean cuisine in this saucy chicken dish.

4	(4-ounce) skinless, boneless chicken breast halves
	Cooking spray
1	tablespoon bottled minced garlic
1	(14.5-ounce) can diced tomatoes with basil, garlic, and oregano, undrained
¼	cup sliced pitted kalamata olives or sliced ripe olives
¼	teaspoon black pepper
¾	cup (3 ounces) crumbled reduced-fat feta cheese

1. Place a large nonstick skillet over medium-high heat. Coat chicken breasts with cooking spray; place in pan. Cook 3 minutes on each side or until browned. Add garlic; sauté 1 minute. Reduce heat to medium; add tomatoes, olives, and pepper. Cook 10 to 15 minutes or until chicken is done. Remove from heat, and sprinkle with feta cheese. Yield: 4 servings (serving size: 1 chicken breast and about ⅓ cup sauce).

POINTS:
5

exchanges:
2 Vegetable
4 Very Lean Meat
½ Lean Meat

per serving:
Calories 226
Carbohydrate 11.8g
Fat 5.3g (saturated 2.3g)
Fiber 1.6g
Protein 32.6g
Cholesterol 73mg
Sodium 971mg
Calcium 153mg
Iron 2.7mg

Shortcut

Olive Options: Quickly chop any remaining olives and store in an airtight container in the refrigerator. Next time a recipe calls for olives, such as Grilled Halibut with Olive Salsa (page 32), you'll have some ready to go. Or toss them on a simple salad or pasta dish for a little added flavor.

prep: 5 minutes   **cook:** 7 minutes

LEMON TURKEY CUTLETS

Fresh lemon juice adds a zesty twist to these tender cutlets. Serve them with Garlic-Roasted Green Beans (page 148) and Roasted Rosemary Potatoes (page 151) for a 9-**POINT** meal.

POINTS:
6

exchanges:
½ Starch
3½ Lean Meat

per serving:
Calories 238
Carbohydrate 6.9g
Fat 11.5g (saturated 2.7g)
Fiber 0.4g
Protein 25.4g
Cholesterol 74mg
Sodium 460mg
Calcium 19mg
Iron 1.9mg

3   tablespoons all-purpose flour

½   teaspoon salt

½   teaspoon ground black pepper

6   (2-ounce) turkey breast cutlets

2   teaspoons olive oil, divided

2   tablespoons fresh lemon juice

Lemon slices (optional)

1. Combine first 3 ingredients in a shallow dish.

2. Rinse turkey cutlets and pat dry. Dredge in flour mixture, shaking off any excess flour; set aside.

3. Heat 1 teaspoon oil in a large nonstick skillet over medium heat. Add 3 cutlets; cook 3 minutes or until lightly browned, turning once. Remove cutlets to a warm serving platter. Repeat procedure with remaining oil and turkey.

4. Sprinkle cutlets with lemon juice. Garnish with lemon slices, if desired. Yield: 3 servings (serving size: 2 cutlets).

Shortcut

Perfectly Browned Cutlets: Use paper towels to quickly absorb the moisture on the cutlets. It's important that the cutlets be dry before dredging in the flour. You want a thin dusting of flour, not a coating—just enough to help brown.

Make Ahead Meals

prep: 5 minutes   **cook:** 30 minutes   **chill:** up to 24 hours

POPPY SEED CHICKEN CASSEROLE

We've taken our favorite creamy chicken casserole and lightened it so you can enjoy its rich flavor and crispy topping with family and friends for a fraction of the **POINTS**.

POINTS:
7

exchanges:
1 Starch
4½ Very Lean Meat
1½ Fat

per serving:
Calories 314
Carbohydrate 17.1g
Fat 10.9g (saturated 5.3g)
Fiber 0.3g
Protein 32.9g
Cholesterol 99mg
Sodium 613mg
Calcium 129mg
Iron 1.5mg

2½ cups chopped cooked chicken breast
¼ teaspoon salt
¼ teaspoon black pepper
1 tablespoon poppy seeds
1 (8-ounce) carton low-fat sour cream
1 (10¾-ounce) can condensed reduced-fat, reduced-sodium cream of chicken soup, undiluted
Butter-flavored cooking spray
10 reduced-fat round buttery crackers, crushed

1. Combine first 6 ingredients in a large bowl, stirring until well blended. Spoon into a 1-quart casserole coated with cooking spray. Cover and refrigerate up to 24 hours.

2. Preheat oven to 350°.

3. Top with crushed crackers. Coat crackers with cooking spray. Bake at 350° for 30 minutes or until thoroughly heated. Yield: 4 servings (serving size: ¾ cup).

Shortcut

Deli-Roasted Chicken: Use an already prepared rotisserie chicken from the deli for the chopped cooked chicken. Make sure to remove the skin. One rotisserie chicken yields about 2½ cups of meat—just the right amount for this recipe.

prep: 13 minutes   **cook:** 9 minutes   **chill:** 2 hours

PASTA SALAD WITH FRESH VEGETABLES

This pasta salad is best made ahead to give the flavors time to blend. The flavors of the lemon and dill dressing with tender chicken and crunchy fresh vegetables are very satisfying.

1½ cups uncooked fusilli

1   cup chopped cooked chicken breast

⅓   cup chopped celery (about 1 stalk)

1   cup grape tomatoes

1   cup chopped seeded cucumber (about 1 medium)

½   cup (2 ounces) crumbled light feta cheese

¼   cup fat-free lemon and dill dressing

¼   teaspoon salt

¼   teaspoon coarsely ground black pepper

1. Cook pasta according to package directions, omitting salt and fat; drain and rinse with cool water. Drain well.

2. Combine cooled pasta and remaining ingredients; toss gently to coat. Chill 2 hours. Yield: 4 servings (serving size: 1⅓ cups).

LOW **POINTS:**

4

exchanges:

1½ Starch
1 Vegetable
2½ Very Lean Meat

per serving:

Calories 226
Carbohydrate 29.3g
Fat 4.1g (saturated 1.8g)
Fiber 2.0g
Protein 18.7g
Cholesterol 35mg
Sodium 425mg
Calcium 82mg
Iron 1.5mg

Shortcut

Prepare a Little Extra: When a recipe calls for pasta, always cook extra; drain well, and spray lightly with cooking spray to prevent sticking. Store in an airtight container in the refrigerator for 1 to 2 days. Reheat noodles in the microwave with a few drops of water to help rehydrate.

prep: 12 minutes   **cook:** 35 minutes   **chill:** up to 8 hours

ITALIAN CHICKEN ROLLUPS

Make these rollups early in the day or the night before. All you'll have to do is pop them
in the oven when you're ready to feast on tender chicken drenched
in marinara sauce and oozing with melted cheese.

POINTS:

5

exchanges:
4 Very Lean Meat
1 Medium-Fat Meat

per serving:
Calories 238
Carbohydrate 6.8g
Fat 8.5g (saturated 3.9g)
Fiber 0.7g
Protein 35.4g
Cholesterol 81mg
Sodium 707mg
Calcium 248mg
Iron 1.5mg

4   (4-ounce) skinless, boneless chicken breast halves

1   teaspoon dried basil

¼   teaspoon salt

¼   teaspoon pepper

4   (1-ounce) part-skim mozzarella string cheese sticks

Cooking spray

1   cup garlic-and-herb tomato sauce

1. Place each chicken breast half between 2 sheets of heavy-duty plastic wrap; pound to ¼-inch thickness, using a meat mallet or rolling pin.

2. Combine basil, salt, and pepper; sprinkle half of mixture evenly over both sides of chicken.

3. Place 1 string cheese stick across the center of each flattened chicken breast. Roll up chicken, jelly roll fashion, starting with short side. Place chicken rollups, seam sides down, in an 11 x 7-inch baking dish. Sprinkle with remaining half of spice mixture, and coat with cooking spray. Cover and refrigerate up to 8 hours.

4. Preheat oven to 350°.

5. Pour tomato sauce over chicken. Bake, uncovered, at 350° for 35 minutes or until chicken is done and tomato sauce is thoroughly heated. Yield: 4 servings (serving size: 1 rollup).

Shortcut

Stock Up on String Cheese: Keep mozzarella string cheese sticks in your refrigerator for a snack or as a quick surprise filling for these chicken rollups.

prep: 2 minutes   **cook:** 19 minutes   **freeze:** up to 6 weeks

CHILI CON CARNE

While the chili is simmering, make a batch of low-fat cornbread muffins, or try some Cheesy Chili Breadsticks (page 145).

Cooking spray

1   pound ground beef, extra lean

1½ cups water

2   teaspoons chipotle chili powder

1   (10-ounce) package frozen chopped onion, celery, and
    bell pepper seasoning mix

1   (16-ounce) can chili beans, undrained

1   (14.5-ounce) can diced tomatoes, undrained

5   tablespoons reduced-fat sour cream

POINTS:

6

exchanges:
1½ Starch
3 Lean Meat

per serving:
Calories 291
Carbohydrate 23.2g
Fat 10.3g (saturated 4.4g)
Fiber 5.7g
Protein 24.8g
Cholesterol 38mg
Sodium 469mg
Calcium 82mg
Iron 3.6mg

1. Place a large saucepan coated with cooking spray over medium-high heat. Add beef; cook 4 minutes or until browned, stirring constantly. Add water, chili powder, frozen vegetable mix, chili beans, and tomatoes; bring to a boil. Reduce heat and simmer, uncovered, 15 minutes, stirring occasionally. Serve immediately or freeze and reheat when ready to serve. Spoon hot chili into individual bowls. Top each serving with 1 tablespoon sour cream. Yield: 5 servings (serving size: 1¼ cups chili and 1 tablespoon sour cream).

Shortcut

Be Prepared: This recipe freezes well, so prepare it to serve on an evening when you don't have time to cook. Just cool chili completely and freeze in a large airtight container or in individual containers for up to 6 weeks. We like zip-top freezer bags and plastic containers with snap lids for storing. Thaw and reheat before serving.

prep: 1 minute   **cook:** 34 minutes   **chill:** up to 8 hours

CHEESY TACO SUPREME

Capture the flavors of a taco or enchilada with crunchy nacho chips, seasoned beef, and rich enchilada sauce. Serve with spicy salsa for an extra kick.

POINTS:
7

exchanges:
1½ Starch
3½ Lean Meat

per serving:
Calories 309
Carbohydrate 20.3g
Fat 14.3g (saturated 6.3g)
Fiber 1.7g
Protein 25.1g
Cholesterol 44mg
Sodium 815mg
Calcium 240mg
Iron 2.3mg

1   pound ground beef, extra lean

½   cup frozen chopped onion

1   (1.25-ounce) package 40%-less-sodium taco seasoning

1   (8-ounce) can no-salt-added tomato sauce

1   (10-ounce) can enchilada sauce

1¼ cups (5 ounces) reduced-fat shredded Cheddar cheese, divided

3   ounces low-fat baked nacho cheese-flavored tortilla chips, crushed (about 1½ cups crushed)

Cooking spray

1. Cook beef and onion in a large skillet over medium-high heat, stirring until beef crumbles and onion is tender; drain well.

2. Return meat mixture to pan; stir in taco seasoning, tomato sauce, and enchilada sauce. Layer half of meat mixture, half of cheese, and half of tortilla chips in an 11 x 7-inch baking dish coated with cooking spray. Repeat layers with remaining meat mixture and cheese. Cover and chill up to 8 hours.

3. Preheat oven to 350°.

4. Bake, covered, at 350° for 20 minutes. Uncover, sprinkle with remaining chips, and bake an additional 9 minutes or until thoroughly heated. Yield: 6 servings (serving size: ⅙ of casserole).

Shortcut

Timesaver: Keep a well-stocked and organized pantry. It's guaranteed to make your time in the kitchen easier, and you will be able to quickly find the ingredients you need when preparing a last minute or make ahead meal.

Herbed Bread Knots,
page 144

Roasted Red Bell
Pepper Hummus,
page 185

Warm Cinnamon Swirls,
page 175

prep: 7 minutes   **cook:** 50 minutes   **chill:** up to 8 hours   **stand:** 5 minutes

HAM AND GRITS CASSEROLE

Sweet ham and cheesy grits make this down-home favorite a simply irresistible breakfast or brunch. Serve with Warm Cinnamon Swirls, pictured on opposite page (recipe on page 175).

4	cups water
½	teaspoon salt
1	cup uncooked quick-cooking grits
2	cups diced 96%-fat-free ham
1	cup (4 ounces) reduced-fat shredded extra-sharp Cheddar cheese
3	tablespoons light butter
1	teaspoon low-sodium Worcestershire sauce
1	cup egg substitute
	Cooking spray

1. Combine water and salt in a large saucepan; bring to a boil. Stir in grits; cover, reduce heat, and simmer 5 minutes or until grits are thick, stirring occasionally. Remove from heat. Add ham and next 3 ingredients; stir until butter melts. Gradually add egg substitute, stirring well.

2. Spoon grits mixture into an 11 x 7-inch baking dish coated with cooking spray. Cook immediately or cover and refrigerate up to 8 hours.

3. Preheat oven to 350°.

4. Bake, uncovered, at 350° for 45 minutes. Let stand 5 minutes before serving. Yield: 6 servings (serving size: 1 cup).

POINTS:
5

exchanges:
1½ Starch
2½ Lean Meat

per serving:
Calories 226
Carbohydrate 22.1g
Fat 7.9g (saturated 4.7g)
Fiber 0.4g
Protein 17.6g
Cholesterol 38mg
Sodium 838mg
Calcium 188mg
Iron 1.3mg

Shortcut

Egg Substitute: Forget the mess of cracking eggs by using fat-free, cholesterol-free egg substitute. One-fourth cup of egg substitute is equal to one egg or two egg whites.

prep: 10 minutes   **cook:** 30 minutes   **chill:** 8 hours   **stand:** 10 minutes

MAPLE-CINNAMON BREAD PUDDING

This is a perfect breakfast dish to serve to weekend guests because you prepare it the night before and bake it the next morning. Serve with fresh strawberries and fat-free milk for a special 8-**POINT** breakfast.

POINTS:
5

exchanges:
2½ Starch
1 Medium-Fat Meat

per serving:
Calories 263
Carbohydrate 38.3g
Fat 8.7g (saturated 4.0g)
Fiber 3.8g
Protein 11.7g
Cholesterol 18mg
Sodium 383mg
Calcium 154mg
Iron 1.9mg

Butter-flavored cooking spray

8   (1-ounce) slices cinnamon-raisin bread, cut into 1-inch cubes

4   ounces Neufchatel cheese, softened

¼   cup bottled cinnamon-sugar, divided

⅛   teaspoon salt

2   cups 1% low-fat milk

¾   cup egg substitute

¼   cup maple syrup

1. Coat an 11 x 7-inch baking dish with cooking spray. Arrange bread cubes in dish.

2. Place Neufchatel cheese, 3 tablespoons cinnamon-sugar, and salt in a bowl; beat with a mixer at medium speed until creamy. Gradually add milk, beating until smooth. Stir in egg substitute and syrup. Pour mixture over bread. Cover and chill 8 hours.

3. Preheat oven to 375°.

4. Uncover dish; sprinkle bread mixture with remaining 1 tablespoon cinnamon-sugar. Bake at 375° for 30 to 32 minutes or until set. Let stand 10 minutes before serving. Yield: 6 servings (serving size: ⅙ of bread pudding).

Shortcut

Clever Cutting: Use a pizza cutter to quickly cut the cinnamon-raisin bread into 1-inch cubes.

Dinners for Two

prep: 3 minutes   **cook:** 7 minutes

ASPARAGUS AND BASIL OMELET

For a quick, light supper, pair this omelet with fresh fruit and a glass of
fat-free milk for a 7-**POINT** meal.

LOW **POINTS:**
4

exchanges:
1 Vegetable
2½ Very Lean Meat
1 Medium-Fat Meat

per serving:
Calories 172
Carbohydrate 5.4g
Fat 8.9g (saturated 4.0g)
Fiber 1.6g
Protein 17.7g
Cholesterol 225mg
Sodium 812mg
Calcium 195mg
Iron 2.6mg

Cooking spray

12   asparagus spears, diagonally cut into 1-inch pieces
     (about 1 cup)

2   large eggs

½   cup egg substitute

¼   cup water

½   teaspoon salt

¼   teaspoon coarsely ground black pepper

2   tablespoons chopped fresh basil

¼   cup (1 ounce) shredded Swiss cheese

1. Heat a nonstick skillet coated with cooking spray over medium-
high heat. Add asparagus, and sauté 3 minutes; set aside.

2. Combine eggs and next 4 ingredients in a medium bowl;
whisk until blended.

3. Wipe pan with paper towels; recoat with cooking spray and
heat over medium heat. Add egg mixture, and cook 3 minutes or
until set (do not stir). Sprinkle with asparagus, basil, and cheese.
Loosen omelet with spatula; fold in half. Cook 1 to 2 minutes or
until egg mixture is set and cheese melts. Slide omelet onto a
plate. Cut in half. Yield: 2 servings (serving size: ½ omelet).

Shortcut

No Separating: Use fat-free, cholesterol-free egg substitute
to add volume to the omelet. This ingredient is a great time
saver because it takes the place of separating egg whites.

prep: 4 minutes   **cook:** 11 minutes

SPICY THAI TOFU

Make a quick stop on the ethnic foods aisle of your supermarket to find canned light coconut milk, chili garlic paste, and Thai peanut sauce.

½   (15-ounce) package extra-firm tofu

1   tablespoon low-sodium soy sauce

Cooking spray

¼   teaspoon chili garlic paste

½   cup light coconut milk

1   cup packaged matchstick carrots

¼   cup Thai peanut sauce

¼   cup diagonally sliced green onions (about 1 large)

1. Slice tofu into 4 (½-inch) slices; place between several layers of paper towels. Place a cutting board on top and press down to remove as much water as possible; pat dry. Brush both sides of tofu lightly with soy sauce.

2. Heat a large nonstick skillet coated with cooking spray over medium-high heat. Add tofu and cook 2 minutes on each side or until golden brown. Remove from pan; set aside.

3. Add chili paste, coconut milk, and carrots to pan; bring to a boil and simmer 5 minutes or until carrots are just tender. Stir in peanut sauce and cook 1 minute. Add tofu and cook 1 minute or until thoroughly heated. Sprinkle with green onions. Yield: 2 servings (serving size: 2 slices tofu and ¼ cup sauce).

POINTS:
5

exchanges:
1 Starch
1 Vegetable
2 Lean Meat
1 Fat

per serving:
Calories 252
Carbohydrate 20.6g
Fat 12.4g (saturated 3.8g)
Fiber 3.2g
Protein 14.3g
Cholesterol 0mg
Sodium 1041mg
Calcium 102mg
Iron 2.7mg

Shortcut

Quick Press: Pressing tofu removes the excess moisture that would otherwise be released during cooking. Use your hands to press the tofu as described in the procedure above, or try using household objects like a gallon jug of water, a heavy skillet, or a heavy can so you can prepare other parts of the meal while the tofu drains.

prep: 3 minutes   **cook:** 15 minutes

MOROCCAN-ROASTED SALMON

Capture the essence of Moroccan-style cooking by serving this salmon
over a bed of couscous or rice.

POINTS:
5

exchanges:
5 Very Lean Meat

per serving:
Calories 220
Carbohydrate 3.4g
Fat 6.4g (saturated 1.3g)
Fiber 0.3g
Protein 35.6g
Cholesterol 90mg
Sodium 869mg
Calcium 80mg
Iron 1.4mg

¼   cup plain low-fat yogurt

1½ teaspoons fresh lime juice

1   teaspoon chopped fresh mint

⅛   teaspoon salt

Olive oil-flavored cooking spray

2   (6-ounce) salmon fillets

2   lime wedges

1   teaspoon Moroccan seasoning (such as The Spice Hunter)

½   teaspoon salt

1. Preheat oven to 400°.

2. Combine yogurt, lime juice, mint, and ⅛ teaspoon salt; set aside.

3. Line broiler pan with foil; coat with cooking spray. Place fish
on broiler pan. Squeeze lime juice from lime wedges over fish.
Sprinkle fish with Moroccan seasoning and ½ teaspoon salt; coat
with cooking spray. Bake at 400° for 15 minutes or until fish
flakes easily when tested with a fork. Serve with yogurt sauce.
Yield: 2 servings (serving size: 1 salmon fillet and 2 tablespoons
yogurt sauce).

Shortcut

Buy the Blend: Spice blends help save time, money, and
cabinet space. Moroccan seasoning combines turmeric,
cinnamon, cumin, fennel, peppermint, clove, basil, and
cayenne for an authentic taste.

prep: 7 minutes   **cook:** 11 minutes

GRILLED TUNA AND ASPARAGUS SALAD
photo, page 101

We loved the taste of fresh grilled tuna and crispy asparagus in this refreshing summer salad.
Enjoy with a glass of Sparkling Fruit Juice Cooler (page 179).

1¼ cups water

16   asparagus spears, diagonally cut into 1-inch pieces

2   (6-ounce) fresh tuna steaks

¼   teaspoon salt

¼   teaspoon pepper

Cooking spray

½   cup diced cucumber

¾   cup chopped tomato (1 small)

3   tablespoons fat-free red wine vinaigrette dressing

POINTS:
5

exchanges:
2 Vegetable
5 Very Lean Meat

per serving:
Calories 256
Carbohydrate 16.2g
Fat 2.1g (saturated 0.5g)
Fiber 3.2g
Protein 42.9g
Cholesterol 77mg
Sodium 594mg
Calcium 61mg
Iron 2.6mg

1. Prepare grill.

2. Bring water to a boil in a medium saucepan; add asparagus.
Reduce heat, and simmer 3 minutes or until crisp-tender. Drain
and rinse with cold water. Place on paper towels.

3. Sprinkle tuna with salt and pepper. Place tuna on grill rack
coated with cooking spray; cook 4 to 5 minutes on each side or
until fish flakes easily when tested with a fork. Flake tuna into
large pieces with fork.

4. Combine asparagus, tuna, cucumber, and tomato; add vinaigrette
and toss gently. Yield: 2 servings (serving size: about 1⅔ cups).

Shortcut

Don't Slip Up: Place a damp cloth or paper towel under
your cutting board when chopping the asparagus, cucumber,
and tomato to keep the board from slipping.

prep: 3 minutes   **cook:** 8 minutes

HERBED SEA SCALLOPS

The chopped parsley and chives serve a dual role. They brighten the flavor and add visual interest to the scallops.

LOW **POINTS:**
3

exchanges:
½ Starch
3 Very Lean Meat

per serving:
Calories 155
Carbohydrate 5.6g
Fat 5.5g (saturated 0.7g)
Fiber 0.3g
Protein 20.0g
Cholesterol 37mg
Sodium 430mg
Calcium 36mg
Iron 0.6mg

1	tablespoon Italian-seasoned breadcrumbs
⅛	teaspoon salt
⅛	teaspoon freshly ground black pepper
½	pound sea scallops
2	teaspoons olive oil
1	tablespoon finely chopped fresh flat-leaf parsley
1	tablespoon chopped fresh chives

1. Place breadcrumbs, salt, and pepper in a zip-top plastic bag. Add scallops; seal and shake gently to coat scallops.

2. Heat oil in a large nonstick skillet over medium-high heat. Add scallops and cook 3 to 4 minutes on each side or until done.

3. Divide scallops between 2 plates; sprinkle evenly with parsley and chives. Serve immediately. Yield: 2 servings (serving size: about 7 scallops).

Shortcut

Chop It Up: Instead of meticulously pulling parsley leaves off the stem, simply cut the stems as close to the leaves as possible with a chef's knife or pair of kitchen shears. Since parsley stems are relatively tender, a few won't be too noticeable. Store extra parsley in a bunch in the refrigerator. Wrap a damp paper towel around the stems to keep the parsley fresh longer.

FRIED SCALLOPS WITH CHILI MAYONNAISE
photo, page 102

Sweet, crispy scallops are delicious when served with mixed greens and chili mayonnaise.

3	tablespoons reduced-fat mayonnaise
1½	tablespoons chili sauce
½	pound sea scallops
¼	teaspoon salt
⅛	teaspoon freshly ground black pepper
1	tablespoon Italian-seasoned breadcrumbs
2	teaspoons olive oil

1. Stir together mayonnaise and chili sauce in a small bowl. Set aside.

2. Combine scallops and next 3 ingredients in a zip-top plastic bag; seal and shake to coat.

3. Heat olive oil in a nonstick skillet over medium-high heat. Add scallops; cook 3 minutes on each side. Serve immediately with chili mayonnaise. Yield: 2 servings (serving size: about 7 scallops and 2 tablespoons chili mayonnaise).

POINTS:
6

exchanges:
½ Starch
3 Very Lean Meat
2 Fat

per serving:
Calories 245
Carbohydrate 10.8g
Fat 13.1g (saturated 1.9g)
Fiber 0.2g
Protein 19.6g
Cholesterol 45mg
Sodium 1103mg
Calcium 37mg
Iron 0.5mg

Shortcut

Even Coating: Dry scallops on a paper towel before coating with breadcrumbs. Use a zip-top plastic bag instead of a bowl to coat the scallops. You'll use fewer breadcrumbs, get a more even coating, and have one less bowl to wash.

THAI-STYLE SHRIMP

If you're hungry for Thai food, satisfy your craving with these saucy shrimp smothered in an authentic Thai-style peanut sauce. You can use the remaining Thai peanut sauce in Spicy Thai Tofu (page 89).

POINTS:
6

exchanges:
2 Starch
4½ Very Lean Meat

per serving:
Calories 308
Carbohydrate 29.2g
Fat 5.5g (saturated 1.1g)
Fiber 2.4g
Protein 32.3g
Cholesterol 242mg
Sodium 1219mg
Calcium 75mg
Iron 5.3mg

Cooking spray
¾ pound peeled and deveined large shrimp
3 cups snow peas, cut in half diagonally
3 garlic cloves, minced
⅓ cup Thai peanut sauce
¼ cup fresh basil leaves, thinly sliced
1 cup hot cooked rice

1. Heat a large nonstick skillet coated with cooking spray over medium-high heat. Add shrimp, snow peas, and garlic. Stir-fry 4 minutes; stir in peanut sauce. Stir-fry 1 minute or until shrimp turn pink and sauce begins to thicken. Remove from heat; stir in basil. Serve over rice. Yield: 2 servings (serving size: 1½ cups shrimp and ½ cup rice).

Shortcut

Shelled Shrimp Conversion: To decrease prep time, we've called for peeled and deveined raw shrimp, available in the seafood market or at the seafood counter of your grocery store. If you prefer to buy shrimp in the shell, you'll need to purchase about 1 pound for this recipe.

BEEF TENDERLOIN WITH MUSTARD-WINE SAUCE

photo, page 103

Accompany these tender pieces of beef with roasted potato wedges and
Roasted Asparagus (page 147).

¼   cup low-salt beef broth

¼   cup dry red wine

1½ teaspoons spicy brown mustard

¾   teaspoon all-purpose flour

¼   teaspoon salt

⅛   teaspoon freshly ground black pepper

Cooking spray

2   (4-ounce) beef tenderloin steaks (about 1 inch thick),
     trimmed

POINTS:
5

exchanges:
3½ Lean Meat

per serving:
Calories 207
Carbohydrate 2.2g
Fat 8.1g (saturated 3.0g)
Fiber 0.5g
Protein 24.2g
Cholesterol 57mg
Sodium 468mg
Calcium 15mg
Iron 3.4mg

1. Combine first 6 ingredients in a small bowl; stir with a whisk.
Set aside.

2. Heat a 10-inch nonstick skillet coated with cooking spray
over medium-high heat. Add steaks; cook 4 minutes on each side
or until desired degree of doneness. Remove to serving plates.

3. Add broth mixture to pan; bring to a boil, scraping pan to
loosen browned bits. Cook until reduced to about ¼ cup (about
30 seconds). Spoon sauce evenly over steaks. Yield: 2 servings
(serving size: 1 steak and 2 tablespoons sauce).

Shortcut

Pass the Wine: There's no need to open another bottle of
red wine for this recipe. Just use ¼ cup of the wine you
plan to serve with the meal.

prep: 6 minutes   **cook:** 7 minutes

FILET OF SIRLOIN WITH ROASTED PEPPERS

For meat lovers, there's nothing more satisfying than a simply-seasoned
sirloin filet served with a crisp green salad.

LOW **POINTS:**
3

exchanges:
1 Vegetable
3 Very Lean Meat

per serving:
Calories 151
Carbohydrate 6.5g
Fat 4.6g (saturated 1.4g)
Fiber 0.9g
Protein 21.1g
Cholesterol 53mg
Sodium 990mg
Calcium 23mg
Iron 1.7mg

½   cup fat-free, less-sodium chicken broth

1   tablespoon tomato paste

¼   teaspoon dried thyme

⅛   teaspoon freshly ground black pepper

½   pound peppercorn flavor beef filet of sirloin (such as
     Hormel), trimmed

Cooking spray

⅓   cup thinly sliced bottled roasted red bell peppers

1. Combine first 4 ingredients in a small bowl; stir with a whisk.

2. Remove beef from packet, discard marinade. Cut beef crosswise into 4
slices. Place beef slices between 2 sheets of heavy-duty plastic wrap;
pound to ½-inch thickness, using a meat mallet or rolling pin. Coat beef
with cooking spray.

3. Place a nonstick skillet over medium-high heat. Add beef; cook 2
minutes on each side. Remove from pan and place on serving plates. Add
roasted bell pepper strips and broth mixture to pan. Bring to a boil. Boil,
stirring constantly, 2 to 3 minutes or until slightly thick. Spoon sauce over
fillets. Yield: 2 servings (serving size: 2 slices beef and ¼ cup sauce).

Shortcut

Save the Extras: Pre-marinated packages of beef weigh
approximately 1 pound. Since this recipe only calls for ½
pound of meat, store the remaining meat in the refrigerator
for up to 3 days or in the freezer for up to 6 months. Slice
filet into ½-inch slices before freezing and store in individual
servings.

prep: 6 minutes   **cook:** 11 minutes

VEAL CHOPS WITH PORTOBELLO SAUCE

Tender veal chops smothered in a rich portobello sauce are delicious
when served with hot cooked rice or crusty French bread.

½ teaspoon dried thyme, divided

½ teaspoon salt, divided

¼ teaspoon freshly ground black pepper

2 (6-ounce) lean center-cut veal loin chops
   (about ½ inch thick)

Cooking spray

1 (6-ounce) package sliced portobello mushrooms,
   coarsely chopped

¼ cup frozen chopped onion

¼ cup beef broth

LOW POINTS:
3

exchanges:
3 Lean Meat

per serving:
Calories 160
Carbohydrate 5.2g
Fat 3.7g (saturated 1.0g)
Fiber 1.7g
Protein 22.0g
Cholesterol 79mg
Sodium 924mg
Calcium 27mg
Iron 1.1mg

1. Sprinkle ¼ teaspoon thyme, ¼ teaspoon salt, and pepper over
veal chops.

2. Heat a large nonstick skillet coated with cooking spray over
medium-high heat. Add chops, and cook 2 to 3 minutes on each
side. Transfer to a plate and keep warm.

3. Add mushrooms, onion, and remaining thyme and salt to pan.
Cook 3 minutes, stirring occasionally. Add broth, and cook 3
minutes or until mushrooms are tender.

4. Return chops to pan; cook 1 to 2 minutes or until thoroughly
heated. Serve immediately. Yield: 2 servings (serving size: 1 chop and
⅓ cup mushroom mixture).

Shortcut

Skip the Knife, Try This: Keep a food chopper on the counter
to make short work out of chopping vegetables. Mini food
choppers are especially good for chopping small amounts of
veggies like celery, carrots, and onion.

prep: 2 minutes   **cook:** 10 minutes

CURRIED PORK CHOPS

Curry powder and red pepper give these pork chops a burst of flavor.

LOW POINTS:
4

exchanges:
3 Lean Meat

per serving:
Calories 165
Carbohydrate 3.9g
Fat 5.2g (saturated 1.7g)
Fiber 0.4g
Protein 24.2g
Cholesterol 72mg
Sodium 334mg
Calcium 20mg
Iron 1.2mg

½ teaspoon curry powder

⅛ teaspoon salt

⅛ teaspoon ground red pepper

2 (4-ounce) boneless center-cut loin pork chops
(about ½ inch thick)

1 tablespoon hoisin sauce

Cooking spray

Chopped fresh cilantro (optional)

1. Prepare grill.

2. Sprinkle curry powder, salt, and pepper over pork chops. Spread hoisin sauce evenly over both sides of pork chops.

3. Place pork on grill rack coated with cooking spray; cover and grill 4 to 5 minutes on each side or until pork is no longer pink. Sprinkle with cilantro, if desired. Yield: 2 servings (serving size: 1 chop).

Shortcut

Buy in Bulk: Buy lean boneless pork chops when they're at a low price. Wrap individually in plastic wrap and freeze. You'll only have to thaw the number of chops you need to cook. Remove chops from the freezer in the morning and place in the refrigerator. The meat should be thawed when you get home from work.

prep: 3 minutes   **cook:** 8 minutes

ITALIAN-STYLE PORK TENDERLOIN

This robust tomato sauce and warm mozzarella cheese topping are delicious over chicken, too!
Sop up any remaining sauce with Herbed Bread Knots (page 144).

½   pound pork tenderloin, trimmed

Cooking spray

⅓   cup frozen chopped onion

¼   teaspoon dried Italian seasoning

⅛   teaspoon salt

⅛   teaspoon coarsely ground black pepper

¾   cup cacciatore sauce (such as Newman's Marinara)

¼   cup (1 ounce) shredded part-skim mozzarella cheese

LOW POINTS:
4

exchanges:
1 Vegetable
3 Very Lean Meat
1 Medium-Fat Meat

per serving:
Calories 203
Carbohydrate 4.8g
Fat 7.3g (saturated 2.9g)
Fiber 1.1g
Protein 28.1g
Cholesterol 83mg
Sodium 390mg
Calcium 111mg
Iron 1.8mg

1. Cut pork crosswise into 6 pieces. Place each piece between 2 sheets of heavy-duty plastic wrap; flatten each piece to ½-inch thickness using a meat mallet or rolling pin.

2. Heat a medium-sized nonstick skillet coated with cooking spray over medium-high heat. Add pork and onion; cook 2 minutes on each side or until pork is lightly browned on both sides. Combine Italian seasoning, salt, and pepper; sprinkle over pork and onion. Pour sauce over pork mixture. Cover, reduce heat, and simmer 3 minutes or until pork is done. Sprinkle with cheese; cover and cook 1 minute or until cheese melts. Yield: 2 servings (serving size: 3 pieces pork and ½ cup sauce).

Shortcut

Fast Flattening: Flatten the meat before cooking and shave minutes off the cook time. If you don't have a meat mallet or rolling pin, use the heel of your hand.

prep: 3 minutes   **marinate:** 1 hour   **cook:** 9 minutes

BALSAMIC-GLAZED CHICKEN

These sweet glazed chicken breasts served with Summer Squash Sauté
(page 154) make a memorable 5-**POINT** dinner.

LOW **POINTS:**
4

exchanges:
4 Very Lean Meat
1 Fat

per serving:
Calories 175
Carbohydrate 2.6g
Fat 5.9g (saturated 1.0g)
Fiber 0.0g
Protein 26.2g
Cholesterol 66mg
Sodium 369mg
Calcium 16mg
Iron 0.9mg

2   teaspoons olive oil

1   tablespoon water

1   tablespoon balsamic vinegar

½   teaspoon sugar

¼   teaspoon cornstarch

¼   teaspoon salt

⅛   teaspoon coarsely ground black pepper

2   (4-ounce) skinless, boneless chicken breast halves

Cooking spray

1. Combine first 7 ingredients in a large zip-top plastic bag. Add chicken; seal and marinate in refrigerator at least 1 hour. Remove chicken from bag; reserve marinade.

2. Heat a nonstick skillet coated with cooking spray over medium-high heat. Add chicken; cook 4 minutes on each side or until done. Remove chicken from pan; keep warm.

3. Add vinegar mixture to pan; bring to a boil, scraping pan to loosen browned bits. Cook until reduced to 2 tablespoons (about 45 seconds). Spoon over chicken. Yield: 2 servings (serving size: 1 chicken breast half and 1 tablespoon sauce).

Shortcut

Simple Skillet Sauce: Deglazing the skillet is the quickest way to make a flavorful sauce or gravy for chicken or meat. Pour about ¼ cup of any liquid—wine, vinegar, apple juice, even water—into the hot pan. Bring to a boil, scraping the pan to loosen the browned bits.

Grilled Tuna and
Asparagus Salad,
page 91

Fried Scallops with Chili Mayonnaise, page 93

**Beef Tenderloin
with Mustard-Wine Sauce,
page 95**

**Monte Cristo Sandwiches,
page 110**

prep: 3 minutes   **cook:** 16 minutes

CHICKEN AND MUSHROOM MARSALA

If you prefer a nonalcoholic version of this recipe, try substituting 1 to 2 tablespoons balsamic vinegar and 2 tablespoons more of chicken broth for the Marsala.

¼   cup Marsala wine

⅓   cup fat-free, less-sodium chicken broth

¼   teaspoon salt

⅛   teaspoon freshly ground black pepper

2   (4-ounce) skinless, boneless chicken breast halves

1   teaspoon olive oil

Cooking spray

2   cups presliced mushrooms

1. Combine first 4 ingredients in a small bowl. Place each chicken breast half between 2 sheets of heavy-duty plastic wrap; flatten to ¼-inch thickness using a meat mallet or rolling pin. Heat oil in a nonstick skillet coated with cooking spray over medium-high heat. Add chicken and cook 3 minutes on each side or until done. Remove from pan; keep warm.

2. Add mushrooms to pan; cook 6 minutes or until browned, stirring occasionally. Add Marsala mixture; simmer 4 minutes or until liquid is reduced to about ¼ cup, scraping pan to loosen browned bits. Spoon over chicken. Yield: 2 servings (serving size: 1 chicken breast half and 2 tablespoons sauce).

LOW **POINTS:**
4

exchanges:
1 Vegetable
4 Very Lean Meat

per serving:
Calories 210
Carbohydrate 6.7g
Fat 3.9g (saturated 0.7g)
Fiber 0.9g
Protein 28.8g
Cholesterol 66mg
Sodium 475mg
Calcium 20mg
Iron 1.7mg

Shortcut

Convenient Cartons: Look for chicken broth in resealable cartons next to the canned broth in the grocery store. You can easily use what you need of the broth, reseal the container, and save in the refrigerator for later use.

CREAMY TARRAGON CHICKEN

Serve this chicken with its creamy sauce over ½ cup wild rice or instant brown rice and steamed broccoli for a 5-**POINT** meal.

LOW POINTS:
3

exchanges:
4 Very Lean Meat

per serving:
Calories 152
Carbohydrate 4.2g
Fat 1.4g (saturated 0.4g)
Fiber 0.2g
Protein 26.8g
Cholesterol 66mg
Sodium 768mg
Calcium 37mg
Iron 1.0mg

¼   cup fat-free, less-sodium chicken broth

¼   cup fat-free half-and-half

¾   teaspoon all-purpose flour

¼   teaspoon dried tarragon

½   teaspoon salt, divided

½   teaspoon coarsely ground black pepper, divided

2   (4-ounce) skinless, boneless chicken breast halves

Cooking spray

1. Combine first 4 ingredients, ¼ teaspoon salt, and ¼ teaspoon black pepper in a small bowl; stir well with a whisk. Set aside.

2. Place chicken between 2 sheets of heavy-duty plastic wrap; flatten each piece to ¼-inch thickness, using a meat mallet or rolling pin. Sprinkle both sides of chicken with remaining ¼ teaspoon salt and ¼ teaspoon black pepper. Coat both sides of chicken with cooking spray.

3. Place a large nonstick skillet coated with cooking spray over medium-high heat. Add chicken and cook 3 minutes on each side or until done. Remove from heat; keep warm.

4. Add broth mixture to pan. Bring to a boil; cook, stirring constantly, 2 minutes or until reduced to ¼ cup, scraping pan to loosen browned bits. Serve sauce over chicken. Yield: 2 servings (serving size: 1 chicken breast half and 2 tablespoons sauce).

Shortcut

Extra Broth Basics: Chicken broth is a pantry staple that can be used in a variety of recipes. Since this recipe calls for only ¼ cup of broth, use any remaining broth to cook the rice instead of water. Or freeze in ice cube trays for later use.

CHICKEN AND BLACK BEAN PIZZA

Monterey Jack cheese with jalapeño peppers adds an extra boost of flavor and spice. If you are unable to find this product, substitute ¼ cup shredded light Mexican cheese blend.

¼   cup chunky salsa

1   (6-inch) Italian cheese-flavored pizza crust
    (such as Boboli)

½   cup shredded cooked chicken

½   cup canned black beans, rinsed and drained

¼   cup (1 ounce) shredded 50%-less-fat Monterey Jack
    cheese with jalapeño peppers

2   tablespoons thinly sliced green onions (about 1 small)

1. Preheat oven to 450°.

2. Spread salsa evenly over pizza crust to within ½ inch of edges; arrange chicken over salsa. Spoon beans over chicken and sprinkle with cheese.

3. Place pizza on a baking sheet. Bake at 450° for 10 minutes or until crust is heated and cheese melts. Sprinkle with green onions. Serve immediately. Yield: 2 servings (serving size: ½ pizza).

POINTS:
6

exchanges:
2 Starch
1½ Very Lean Meat
1 Medium-Fat Meat

per serving:
Calories 299
Carbohydrate 34.0g
Fat 8.2g (saturated 3.2g)
Fiber 3.5g
Protein 22.8g
Cholesterol 39mg
Sodium 733mg
Calcium 321mg
Iron 3.0mg

Shortcut

Convenient Crust: Commercial pizza crust is an ideal on hand ingredient when you need to quickly prepare a meal. Because the crust is vacuum packed, it can be stored at room temperature for up to 1 months.

TURKEY AND CELERY BURGERS

These burgers are delicious served on light wheat rolls with the traditional toppings or with cranberry sauce or chutney.

POINTS:
5

exchanges:
3 Lean Meat
½ Fat

per serving:
Calories 206
Carbohydrate 3.4g
Fat 11.7g (saturated 2.9g)
Fiber 0.3g
Protein 20.4g
Cholesterol 90mg
Sodium 527mg
Calcium 25mg
Iron 1.7mg

1	pound ground turkey breast
¼	cup diced celery
2	tablespoons Italian-seasoned breadcrumbs
1½	teaspoons Worcestershire sauce
½	teaspoon salt
¼	teaspoon freshly ground black pepper
2	teaspoons olive oil

Cooking spray

1. Combine first 6 ingredients in a small bowl. Divide meat mixture into 4 equal portions, shaping each into a ½-inch-thick patty.

2. Heat oil in a medium nonstick skillet coated with cooking spray over medium heat. Add patties and cook 4 to 5 minutes on each side or until done. Yield: 4 servings (serving size: 1 burger).

Shortcut

Double Duty Cooking: This recipe makes 4 turkey burgers. Cook 2 for tonight's dinner and wrap the other 2 in plastic wrap and freeze for another meal.

SANTA FE BURGERS

Serve this south-of-the-border favorite with a Tangy Fruit Cocktail
(page 180) and baked tortilla chips.

2   (2.8-ounce) frozen meatless soy protein burgers

2   (1.7-ounce) reduced-calorie whole wheat hamburger buns

2   (¾-ounce) slices 2% Monterey Jack cheese with jalapeño
     peppers

4   thin avocado slices

¼   cup chunky salsa

1. Cook burgers in skillet according to package directions.

2. Place 1 burger on bottom half of each bun; top each with 1
cheese slice, 2 avocado slices, and 2 tablespoons salsa. Cover with
top half of bun. Serve immediately. Yield: 2 servings (serving size:
1 burger).

POINTS:
7

exchanges:
3 Starch
1 Very Lean Meat
1 Medium-Fat Meat

per serving:
Calories 345
Carbohydrate 47.6g
Fat 10.7g (saturated 4.2g)
Fiber 12.8g
Protein 21.8g
Cholesterol 27mg
Sodium 987mg
Calcium 332mg
Iron 1.0mg

Shortcut

Suppertime Soy Solution: Our staff really likes the flavor
and convenience of these soy protein burgers, especially the
Boca Burger and Morningstar Farms brands. They are very
versatile, require little clean up, and can be cooked in the
microwave, toaster oven, or skillet.

MONTE CRISTO SANDWICHES

photo, page 104

The traditional Monte Cristo sandwich is fried and would weigh in at more than 10-**POINTS**. We've lightened this version to only 4-**POINTS**!

LOW **POINTS:**
4

exchanges:
1½ Starch
1 Very Lean Meat
1 Lean Meat

per serving:
Calories 200
Carbohydrate 26.1g
Fat 3.8g (saturated 1.2g)
Fiber 5.0g
Protein 19.5g
Cholesterol 20mg
Sodium 960mg
Calcium 284mg
Iron 2.9mg

4   teaspoons sweetened tangy honey mustard

4   (0.8-ounce) slices light white bread

4   (½-ounce) slices reduced-fat Swiss cheese

2   ounces thinly sliced lean ham

2   tablespoons fat-free milk

1   large egg white

Cooking spray

1   teaspoon powdered sugar

Low-sugar cranberry-raspberry jam (optional)

1. Spread 1 teaspoon mustard over each bread slice. Place 2 cheese slices on each of 2 bread slices. Divide ham evenly over cheese. Cover with remaining bread slices, mustard sides down. Combine milk and egg white in a shallow dish. Quickly dip both sides of each sandwich into milk mixture.

2. Heat a large nonstick skillet coated with cooking spray over medium-high heat. Add sandwiches and cook 3 minutes on each side or until lightly browned. Sprinkle each sandwich with ½ teaspoon sugar. Dollop each with jam, if desired. Serve immediately. Yield: 2 servings (serving size: 1 sandwich).

Shortcut

Easy Egg Separating: Separate the egg white from the yolk quickly by cracking the egg and letting the white run through your fingers into the bowl. Discard the yolk or use immediately in another recipe. Make sure to wash your hands before and after.

prep: 3 minutes   **cook:** 6 minutes

GRILLED MOZZARELLA SANDWICH WITH SPINACH AND PESTO

We've refined the flavors of the traditional grilled cheese sandwich by using creamy mozzarella, fresh spinach, and a hint of pesto.

2   tablespoons light mayonnaise

2   teaspoons pesto

4   (⅔-ounce) slices light wheat bread (such as Pepperidge Farm)

4   (⅔-ounce) slices part-skim mozzarella cheese

12   baby spinach leaves (about ¼ cup)

Butter-flavored cooking spray

POINTS:
6

exchanges:
1½ Starch
2 Medium-Fat Meat

per serving:
Calories 274
Carbohydrate 21.3g
Fat 15.1g (saturated 5.9g)
Fiber 3.5g
Protein 16.2g
Cholesterol 28mg
Sodium 553mg
Calcium 349mg
Iron 1.7mg

1. Combine mayonnaise and pesto in a small bowl. Spread pesto mixture evenly on 1 side of each bread slice. Top each of 2 bread slices with 1 cheese slice, 6 spinach leaves, 1 cheese slice, and 1 bread slice. Coat both sides of sandwich with cooking spray.

2. Heat a large nonstick skillet coated with cooking spray over medium heat. Place sandwiches, coated sides down, in pan; cook 3 minutes on each side or until lightly browned and cheese melts. Yield: 2 servings (serving size: 1 sandwich).

Shortcut

Leave the Stems: There's no need to trim the stems from baby spinach leaves. They're so tender that they cook quickly.

Bacon, Cheese, and Spinach-Stuffed Potatoes

These potatoes are so stuffed with yummy ingredients that they make a whole meal.
They can also be served as a side dish though one potato half makes a hearty 3-**POINT**
accompaniment to beef, pork, or chicken.

POINTS:
6

exchanges:
3 Starch
1 Lean Meat
½ Medium-Fat Meat

per serving:
Calories 308
Carbohydrate 44.7g
Fat 8.0g (saturated 4.5g)
Fiber 4.5g
Protein 16.3g
Cholesterol 40mg
Sodium 748mg
Calcium 225mg
Iron 2.9mg

2   (8-ounce) baking potatoes

2   cups baby spinach leaves

¼   cup low-fat sour cream

¼   teaspoon salt

⅛   teaspoon freshly ground black pepper

¼   cup diced Canadian bacon

¼   cup (1 ounce) reduced-fat shredded sharp Cheddar cheese

1. Pierce potatoes with a fork; arrange on paper towels in a microwave oven. Microwave at HIGH 10 minutes or until tender, turning potatoes after 6 minutes. Let stand 5 minutes.

2. Arrange spinach in a large microwave-safe bowl. While potatoes are standing, cook spinach at HIGH 45 seconds or until wilted.

3. Cut each potato in half lengthwise; scoop out pulp, leaving a ¼-inch-thick shell. Add spinach and next 4 ingredients to potato pulp; mix well.

4. Arrange potato shells on a shallow microwave-safe plate; fill with potato-spinach mixture, mounding, if necessary. Sprinkle with cheese. Microwave at HIGH 1 minute or until cheese melts. Yield: 2 servings (serving size: 2 potato halves).

Shortcut

Easy Scooping: Use a regular teaspoon to easily scoop out the insides of the potato.

Family
Favorite
Recipes

SCRAMBLED EGG BURRITOS

Scrambled eggs aren't just for breakfast anymore. This Mexican-style burrito is hearty enough for lunch or a light dinner.

POINTS:
5

exchanges:
1 Starch
1 Very Lean Meat
1 Medium-Fat Meat
1 Fat

per serving:
Calories 226
Carbohydrate 16.8g
Fat 10.8g (saturated 4.5g)
Fiber 1.6g
Protein 15.8g
Cholesterol 148mg
Sodium 693mg
Calcium 148mg
Iron 2.5mg

4   large eggs

½   cup egg substitute

2   teaspoons finely chopped fresh cilantro

¼   teaspoon salt

½   teaspoon coarsely ground black pepper

½   cup (2 ounces) shredded light Mexican cheese blend, divided (such as Sargento)

2   teaspoons butter

4   (7-inch) flour tortillas, warmed

½   cup salsa

1. Combine first 5 ingredients in a medium bowl; stir well with a whisk. Add ¼ cup cheese; stir.

2. Melt butter in a medium nonstick skillet over medium heat. Reduce heat to medium-low. Add egg mixture, and cook, without stirring, until egg mixture begins to set on bottom. Draw a spatula across bottom of pan to form large curds. Continue cooking until egg mixture is thick but still moist; do not stir constantly. Spoon ½ cup egg mixture evenly down center of each tortilla. Top each with 2 tablespoons salsa and 1 tablespoon cheese; roll up and secure with a toothpick. Yield: 4 servings (serving size: 1 burrito).

Shortcut

Heat a Tortilla: Tortillas can be warmed quickly in a microwave oven by placing up to 4 in an unsealed heavy-duty zip-top plastic bag and microwaving at HIGH for 20 to 25 seconds or until thoroughly heated.

prep: 5 minutes   **cook:** 4 minutes

HOT GRILLED CHEESE AND TOMATO SANDWICHES

Spicy Dijon mustard and thick, juicy tomato slices dress up this version of the
classic grilled cheese sandwich.

1   tablespoon plus 1 teaspoon yogurt-based spread
    (such as Brummel and Brown)
8   (1-ounce) diagonally cut slices Italian bread
2   teaspoons Dijon mustard
8   (¼-inch-thick) tomato slices (about 2)
4   (¾-ounce) slices 2% American cheese (such as Kraft)
Cooking spray

POINTS:
5

exchanges:
2 Starch
1 Medium-Fat Meat

per serving:
Calories 243
Carbohydrate 34.2g
Fat 7.0g (saturated 2.8g)
Fiber 2.2g
Protein 9.8g
Cholesterol 9mg
Sodium 735mg
Calcium 290mg
Iron 2.1mg

1. Spread ½ teaspoon yogurt-based spread evenly over each slice
of bread. Spread ½ teaspoon mustard on other side of 4 slices of
bread. Arrange 2 tomato slices on top of each mustard-coated slice;
top tomato slices with 1 cheese slice, and top with remaining slices
of bread, buttered-side up.

2. Heat a large nonstick skillet coated with cooking spray over
medium-high heat. Add sandwiches, and cook 2 minutes or until
bottom bread slices are lightly browned. Turn sandwiches and
cook 2 minutes or until cheese melts and bottom bread slices are
lightly browned. Serve immediately. Yield: 4 servings (serving
size: 1 sandwich).

Shortcut

Sandwich Assembly: Instead of making each sandwich
individually, use the assembly-line method. Line up the
bread on the counter in 2 parallel rows with bottom edges
of bread touching each other. Then layer the ingredients. It's
an easy way to keep someone from getting shortchanged
on an ingredient.

SPINACH AND MUSHROOM ALFREDO

For even more flavor, add 0-**POINT** vegetables such as onions
and bell pepper to the garlic and mushroom sauté.

POINTS:
6

exchanges:
2½ Starch
1 Vegetable
2 Very Lean Meat

per serving:
Calories 300
Carbohydrate 42.9g
Fat 7.5g (saturated 3.5g)
Fiber 3.9g
Protein 15.0g
Cholesterol 23mg
Sodium 546mg
Calcium 168mg
Iron 2.0mg

1 (9-ounce) package refrigerated fettuccine

Cooking spray

½ teaspoon bottled minced garlic

1 (8-ounce) package presliced mushrooms

1 (10-ounce) container refrigerated light Alfredo sauce

1 (7-ounce) package fresh baby spinach

¼ teaspoon freshly ground black pepper

1. Cook fettuccine according to package directions, omitting salt
and fat. Drain well. Transfer to a large bowl.

2. While pasta cooks, heat a large nonstick skillet coated with
cooking spray over medium-high heat. Add garlic and mushrooms;
sauté 5 minutes or until mushrooms are tender. Add Alfredo sauce,
stirring well. Add spinach; cover and cook 3 minutes or just until
spinach wilts. Remove from heat, and stir.

3. Add Alfredo mixture to pasta; toss well. Sprinkle with black
pepper. Serve immediately. Yield: 4 servings (serving size: about
1 cup).

Shortcut

Open and Cook: No mincing or slicing, and very little
measuring is needed when you use convenience products
from the fresh produce and refrigerated sections of the
supermarket.

prep: 8 minutes   **cook:** 12 minutes

CRISPY BAKED CATFISH

*Enjoy a down-home meal with your family by pairing this oven-fried catfish
with slaw and baked potato wedges.*

4   (6-ounce) catfish fillets

1   teaspoon seafood seasoning (such as Chef Paul Prudhomme's)

½   teaspoon salt

3   large egg whites

1   cup dry breadcrumbs

Cooking spray

Lemon wedges (optional)

1. Preheat oven to 450°.

2. Rinse fillets, and pat dry with paper towels to remove excess moisture. Sprinkle both sides of fillets with seasoning and salt. Lightly beat egg whites in a shallow dish. Place breadcrumbs in a shallow dish. Dip each fillet in egg white and dredge lightly in breadcrumbs. Repeat procedure with remaining egg white and breadcrumbs so that each fillet is dipped twice.

3. Coat a foil-lined baking sheet with cooking spray. Place fish on pan and bake at 450° for 12 minutes or until fish flakes easily when tested with a fork. Serve immediately with lemon wedges, if desired. Yield: 4 servings (serving size: 1 fillet).

POINTS:

6

exchanges:
1½ Starch
4½ Very Lean Meat

per serving:
Calories 285
Carbohydrate 21.1g
Fat 6.3g (saturated 1.6g)
Fiber 0.9g
Protein 33.9g
Cholesterol 99mg
Sodium 713mg
Calcium 92mg
Iron 2.2mg

Shortcut

Breading Secret: When dipping fish into egg mixture and breadcrumbs, use one hand for the wet mixture and the other for the dry ingredients. It will go faster and you'll use fewer breadcrumbs.

prep: 3 minutes   **cook:** 8 minutes

SHRIMP SCAMPI

Enjoy the intense flavor of garlic-infused shrimp with warm angel hair pasta
and a glass of chilled white wine.

LOW POINTS:
4

exchanges:
4 Very Lean Meat
1 Fat

per serving:
Calories 175
Carbohydrate 1.8g
Fat 6.4g (saturated 1.1g)
Fiber 0.2g
Protein 26.3g
Cholesterol 242mg
Sodium 573mg
Calcium 60mg
Iron 4.2mg

1½ tablespoons olive oil

1½ tablespoons bottled minced garlic

1½ pounds peeled and deveined large shrimp

¼ cup finely chopped fresh flat-leaf parsley

1½ tablespoons fresh lemon juice

½ teaspoon salt

⅛ teaspoon ground red pepper

1. Heat oil in a large nonstick skillet over medium-low heat; add garlic, and cook 1 minute. Add shrimp, and cook 5 minutes or until shrimp turn pink, stirring occasionally; remove pan from heat. Stir in parsley and remaining ingredients. Yield: 4 servings (serving size: 1 cup).

Shortcut

Decrease Prep Time: We've used bottled minced garlic and peeled and deveined shrimp from the supermarket to drastically cut the prep time on this recipe. If you prefer to mince your own garlic, it will take 7 cloves to yield 1½ tablespoons minced garlic. Purchase 2¼ pounds of unpeeled shrimp if you prefer to peel and devein your own.

Flash-Pan
Fajitas,
page 128

Mustard-Glazed Pork Chops,
page 129

Oven-Fried Chicken Tenders,
page 136

Pizza Quesadillas,
page 142

MUSHROOM-SMOTHERED SALISBURY STEAK
photo, cover

This is the perfect recipe for unexpected company. Your guests are sure to feel welcome when you serve this down-home recipe with creamy mashed potatoes and crisp green beans.

1	(14-ounce) can beef broth
3	tablespoons flour
½	teaspoon salt, divided
½	cup picante sauce, divided
12	ounces ground beef, extra lean
3	tablespoons Italian-seasoned breadcrumbs
1	large egg white
Cooking spray	
½	(8-ounce) package presliced mushrooms

POINTS:
5

exchanges:
1 Starch
2½ Lean Meat

per serving:
Calories 214
Carbohydrate 11.9g
Fat 8.2g (saturated 3.2g)
Fiber 1.8g
Protein 21.4g
Cholesterol 31mg
Sodium 1052mg
Calcium 21mg
Iron 2.8mg

1. Combine beef broth, flour, and ¼ teaspoon salt in a small bowl; stir with a whisk. Add ¼ cup picante sauce; stir well. Set aside.

2. Combine beef, breadcrumbs, egg white, and remaining picante sauce and salt in a large bowl. Divide mixture into 4 equal portions, shaping each into a ½-inch-thick patty; set aside.

3. Heat a large nonstick skillet coated with cooking spray over medium-high heat. Add patties; cook 5 minutes on each side or until done. Remove from heat; cover, and set aside.

4. Add mushrooms to pan; sauté 2 minutes or until browned. Add reserved broth mixture to pan. Bring to a boil; cook 3 minutes or until slightly thick, stirring constantly. Return patties to pan and cook until thoroughly heated. Yield: 4 servings (serving size: 1 patty and ¼ cup sauce).

Shortcut

Make Ahead: Make the beef patties ahead, wrap in heavy-duty plastic wrap and freeze. Thaw before cooking.

SKILLET SHEPHERD'S PIE

A traditional shepherd's pie takes over 1 hour to prepare and cook.
This recipe takes only 12 minutes from start to finish!

POINTS:
7

exchanges:
1 Starch
1 Vegetable
4 Lean Meat

per serving:
Calories 319
Carbohydrate 16.4g
Fat 14.7g (saturated 6.1g)
Fiber 2.4g
Protein 28.7g
Cholesterol 51mg
Sodium 776mg
Calcium 131mg
Iron 3.1mg

1   pound extra lean ground beef

Cooking spray

1   cup frozen diced green bell pepper

1   tablespoon chili powder

½   teaspoon salt, divided

1   (14-ounce) package refrigerated mashed potatoes (such as Simply Potatoes Country Style Mashed Potatoes)

½   cup (2 ounces) reduced-fat shredded sharp Cheddar cheese

1. Preheat broiler.

2. Cook ground beef in a 10-inch large ovenproof nonstick skillet coated with cooking spray over medium-high heat until browned; stir to crumble. Drain well; return beef to pan. Add frozen bell pepper, chili powder, and ¼ teaspoon salt; cook 3 minutes or until thoroughly heated. Set aside.

3. Prepare potatoes according to package directions, using remaining ¼ teaspoon salt.

4. Spoon potatoes evenly over meat mixture. Sprinkle potatoes evenly with cheese. Broil 2 minutes or until cheese melts. Yield: 4 servings (serving size: ¼ of skillet).

Shortcut

No Need to Thaw: Use frozen mashed potatoes and green bell peppers to cut down on the preparation time. There's no need to thaw the peppers before adding them to the meat in the skillet.

prep: 2 minutes **cook:** 17 minutes

SKILLET STUFFED PEPPERS

With one skillet and less than 20 minutes, you can prepare this complete
meal of vegetables, meat, and rice.

3	large green, red, or yellow bell peppers
12	ounces extra lean ground beef
½	cup picante sauce
½	cup water
1	teaspoon sugar
⅓	cup uncooked instant rice
½	cup (2 ounces) reduced-fat shredded sharp Cheddar cheese

POINTS:
8

exchanges:
1 Starch
3 Vegetable
4 Lean Meat

per serving:
Calories 343
Carbohydrate 21.8g
Fat 14.5g (saturated 6.8g)
Fiber 2.6g
Protein 29.8g
Cholesterol 55mg
Sodium 541mg
Calcium 157mg
Iron 3.4mg

1. Cut peppers in half lengthwise. Discard seeds.

2. Cook ground beef in a large nonstick skillet over medium-
high heat until browned; stir to crumble. Stir in picante sauce
and next 3 ingredients; top with pepper halves, cut side down.
Bring to a boil; cover, reduce heat, and simmer 13 minutes or
until peppers are crisp-tender.

3. Place pepper halves, cut side up, on a serving platter. Spoon
⅓ cup beef mixture into halves. Sprinkle each half with 1 tablespoon cheese. Serve immediately. Yield: 3 servings (serving size:
2 pepper halves).

Shortcut

No Hassle: Eliminate the frustration of stuffed peppers
tipping over in the pan while they cook. We cut down on
the cooking time and solved the tipping problem by cooking
the peppers on top of the stove and stuffing them after
everything is cooked.

FLASH-PAN FAJITAS

photo, page 121

In only 8 minutes, your family can sit down and enjoy these sizzling fajitas
loaded with seasoned beef and crisp vegetables.

POINTS:
5

exchanges:
2 Starch
2 Lean Meat

per serving:
Calories 276
Carbohydrate 30.6g
Fat 5.8g (saturated 1.8g)
Fiber 4.4g
Protein 23.5g
Cholesterol 50mg
Sodium 700mg
Calcium 60mg
Iron 3.5mg

12 ounces boneless sirloin steak, trimmed and thinly sliced across the grain

1½ teaspoons blackened steak seasoning (such as Chef Paul Prudhomme's)

2   teaspoons ground cumin

¼   teaspoon salt

1   (16-ounce) package frozen bell pepper stir-fry (such as Bird's Eye)

Cooking spray

4   (8-inch) 98%-fat-free flour tortillas, warmed (such as Mission)

Fat-free sour cream (optional)

Lime wedges (optional)

1. Combine first 4 ingredients in a medium bowl; toss well.

2. Place bell pepper stir-fry in a colander; rinse with cold water 15 seconds
or until thawed; drain completely, and towel dry.

3. Heat a large nonstick skillet coated with cooking spray over medium-high
heat. Add beef to pan; cook 4 minutes or until done, stirring constantly.

4. Coat pan with cooking spray; add pepper mixture, and cook 2 minutes,
stirring constantly. Add beef, and cook 30 seconds or until thoroughly heated.

5. Place 1 tortilla on each serving plate; spoon ¾ cup beef mixture down
center of each tortilla. Top each with sour cream and squeeze with lime
wedges, if desired. Roll up. Yield: 4 servings (serving size: ¾ cup beef mixture
and 1 tortilla).

Shortcut

Let the Butcher Help: Ask the butcher to thinly slice the sirloin
for you while you complete your grocery shopping. Or place
the uncut meat in the freezer for 10 minutes until it's firm but
not frozen. It will be easier to cut the meat across the grain.

prep: 3 minutes   **cook:** 21 minutes

MUSTARD-GLAZED PORK CHOPS
photo, page 122

Simmered in a tangy mustard and honey sauce, these tender pork chops are irresistible. If you prefer, substitute apple juice for the wine. Serve with steamed broccoli spears and mashed potatoes with chopped green onions for a 9-**POINT** meal.

4	(6-ounce) bone-in center-cut pork chops (about ¾ inch thick)
¼	teaspoon salt
⅛	teaspoon pepper
	Cooking spray
1½	cups dry white wine
⅓	cup honey
¼	cup Dijon mustard

POINTS:
7

exchanges:
1½ Starch
3 Lean Meat

per serving:
Calories 307
Carbohydrate 25.5g
Fat 7.1g (saturated 2.2g)
Fiber 0.3g
Protein 22.5g
Cholesterol 58mg
Sodium 573mg
Calcium 53mg
Iron 1.4mg

1. Sprinkle pork with salt and pepper. Heat a large nonstick skillet coated with cooking spray over medium-high heat. Add pork; cook 3 minutes on each side or until browned. Remove pork from pan.

2. Add wine, honey, and mustard to pan; bring to a boil, and cook 3 minutes.

3. Add pork; reduce heat, and simmer for 12 minutes, turning pork after 6 minutes. Yield: 4 servings (serving size: 1 pork chop and 3 tablespoons sauce).

Shortcut

Multi-Task Tongs: Kitchen tongs are one of the most versatile tools to have in the kitchen. They come in various lengths and can be used for many things—turning meat in the skillet, tossing and serving a salad, or removing a baked potato from the oven.

PORK CHOPS WITH SWEET ORANGE BARBECUE SAUCE

Stir chopped green onions into hot cooked rice for a side dish guaranteed to complement these sweet and saucy chops.

LOW POINTS:
4

exchanges:
½ Starch
3 Lean Meat

per serving:
Calories 181
Carbohydrate 9.0g
Fat 4.9g (saturated 1.7g)
Fiber 0.3g
Protein 24.4g
Cholesterol 71mg
Sodium 328mg
Calcium 21mg
Iron 1.2mg

1   teaspoon grated orange rind

⅓   cup fresh orange juice

3   tablespoons ketchup

1   tablespoon sugar

1   tablespoon low-sodium soy sauce

1   teaspoon bottled chopped ginger

Cooking spray

4   (4-ounce) boneless center-cut loin pork chops

¼   teaspoon freshly ground black pepper

1. Combine first 6 ingredients in a small bowl; set aside.

2. Place a large nonstick skillet coated with cooking spray over medium-high heat. Sprinkle both sides of pork with black pepper. Add pork to pan, and cook 4 minutes on each side. Remove pork from pan, and keep warm.

3. Add orange mixture to pan, scraping pan to loosen browned bits. Bring to a boil; reduce heat to medium and cook 2 minutes or until mixture is reduced to about ¼ cup. Serve sauce over pork. Yield: 4 servings (serving size: 1 pork chop and 1 tablespoon sauce).

Shortcut

Buy It Bottled: Bottled fresh ginger eliminates the time spent peeling and grating fresh ginger. You will find bottled ginger in the produce section of the supermarket. When substituting the bottled ginger for fresh, substitute in equal amounts.

prep: 3 minutes   **cook:** 8 minutes   **stand:** 3 minutes

HAM AND CURRIED PINEAPPLE SAUCE

We loved the sweet and salty flavor combination of the ham and pineapple.
Baked sweet potatoes are a tasty side dish.

4   (3-ounce) slices 33%-less-sodium lean ham

Cooking spray

1   (15¼-ounce) can pineapple tidbits in juice

½   teaspoon curry powder

¼   teaspoon crushed red pepper

2   tablespoons yogurt-based spread (such as Brummel
     and Brown)

1. Coat both sides of ham with cooking spray. Place a large non-stick skillet over medium-high heat until hot. Add ham; cook 1½ to 2 minutes on each side or until lightly browned. Remove ham from pan. Keep warm.

2. Add pineapple, curry, and red pepper to pan. Bring to a boil; cook 4 minutes or until most of liquid has evaporated, stirring constantly. Remove from heat; stir in yogurt-based spread. Cover and let stand 3 minutes to allow flavors to blend.

3. Serve ⅓ cup sauce over each ham slice. Yield: 4 servings (serving size: 1 ham slice and ⅓ cup sauce).

LOW **POINTS:**
4

exchanges:
1 Starch
2 Lean Meat

per serving:
Calories 178
Carbohydrate 17.8g
Fat 5.4g (saturated 1.6g)
Fiber 1.1g
Protein 14.2g
Cholesterol 36mg
Sodium 760mg
Calcium 7mg
Iron 1.7mg

Shortcut

Hassle-Free Ham Steaks: Center-cut ham steaks are sold individually in a vacuum-sealed package in the deli or meat section of the grocery store. Each steak usually weighs about 1 pound. Because the steaks are precooked, it takes only a few minutes to warm them in the skillet. Store leftover ham in the refrigerator in an airtight container for up to 3 days.

prep: 1 minute   **cook:** 15 minutes   **stand:** 3 minutes

PENNE WITH SAUSAGE AND ROASTED PEPPER SAUCE

Give ordinary spaghetti sauce a homemade flavor by adding sausage and roasted red bell peppers.

POINTS:
7

exchanges:
3 Starch
2 Lean Meat

per serving:
Calories 329
Carbohydrate 45.5g
Fat 9.5g (saturated 2.9g)
Fiber 3.1g
Protein 15.0g
Cholesterol 30mg
Sodium 694mg
Calcium 62mg
Iron 3.1mg

2 cups uncooked penne or other tubed-shaped pasta

6 ounces 50%-less-fat pork sausage (such as Jimmy Dean)

1¼ cups bottled spaghetti sauce (such as Classico with mushrooms and ripe olives)

½ cup diced bottled roasted red bell peppers

¾ teaspoon sugar

⅛ teaspoon salt

1. Cook pasta according to package directions, omitting salt and fat. Drain well.

2. While pasta cooks, cook sausage in a large nonstick skillet over medium heat 6 to 8 minutes or until brown; stir to crumble. Drain sausage.

3. Add spaghetti sauce and bell peppers to pan; bring to a boil. Reduce heat and simmer, uncovered, 5 minutes or until slightly thick. Remove from heat; stir in sugar and salt. Cover and let stand 3 minutes. Serve over pasta. Yield: 4 servings (serving size: 1 cup pasta and ½ cup sauce).

Shortcut

Boil Water: Water will come to a rolling boil faster over high heat with the pot lid on. However, once the pasta is added to the water, don't replace the lid. Instead, bring the water back to a boil, and cook, stirring often, until the pasta is done.

CREAMY PEPPER PASTA

Garlic-roasted cream cheese adds an extra burst of flavor to this creamy pasta dish.

3   cups uncooked no-yolk noodles

1   (16-ounce) package frozen bell pepper stir-fry

1½ cups frozen diced cooked chicken breast

¾   cup light cream cheese with roasted garlic

⅓   cup fat-free milk

¾   teaspoon salt

½   teaspoon black pepper

2   tablespoons preshredded fresh Parmesan cheese

POINTS:
7

exchanges:
2½ Starch
1 Vegetable
3 Very Lean Meat
1 Fat

per serving:
Calories 356
Carbohydrate 39.1g
Fat 10.4g (saturated 5.8g)
Fiber 3.0g
Protein 25.9g
Cholesterol 92mg
Sodium 879mg
Calcium 148mg
Iron 2.7mg

1. Cook pasta according to package directions, omitting salt and fat. Add bell pepper stir-fry to pasta water during the last 2 minutes of cooking.

2. Place chicken in a colander. Pour pasta mixture over chicken; drain well.

3. Return pasta mixture to pan. Add cream cheese and next 3 ingredients, stirring until cream cheese melts. Sprinkle with Parmesan cheese. Yield: 4 servings (serving size: about 1⅓ cups).

Shortcut

No Thawing Required: There's no need to thaw the pepper stir-fry or frozen chicken before beginning this recipe. Just add the stir-fry to the noodles the last 2 minutes of cooking time. Place the frozen chicken in the colander and pour the hot water, noodles, and stir-fry over the chicken. By the time the noodles have drained well, the chicken will be hot.

prep: 13 minutes   **cook:** 33 minutes

CHICKEN ENCHILADAS VERDES

The tortillas are dipped in heated broth to soften them so they can be rolled easily.

POINTS:
7

exchanges:
2 Starch
4 Lean Meat

per serving:
Calories 346
Carbohydrate 28.7g
Fat 10.0g (saturated 4.7g)
Fiber 2.1g
Protein 33.6g
Cholesterol 84mg
Sodium 699mg
Calcium 257mg
Iron 1.4mg

2   cups chopped cooked chicken breast

1¼ cups crumbled queso fresco cheese, divided

2   cups bottled salsa verde, divided

2   teaspoons ground cumin

Cooking spray

1   cup fat-free, less-sodium chicken broth

8   (6-inch) corn tortillas

1. Preheat oven to 400°.

2. Combine chicken, ¾ cup cheese, ¾ cup salsa verde, and cumin in a medium bowl.

3. Spread ½ cup salsa verde on bottom of an 11 x 7-inch baking dish coated with cooking spray.

4. Heat chicken broth in a small saucepan. Dip 1 tortilla at a time into hot broth; remove, and spoon ½ cup chicken mixture down center of tortilla. Roll up and place, seam side down, over salsa in baking dish. Repeat with remaining tortillas and chicken mixture.

5. Spoon remaining ¾ cup salsa evenly over enchiladas; sprinkle with remaining ½ cup cheese. Cover with quick-release foil. Bake at 400° for 20 minutes; uncover and bake an additional 10 minutes or until cheese is lightly browned. Yield: 4 servings (serving size: 2 enchiladas).

Shortcut

No-Cling Foil: This recipe is a good candidate for the new quick-release foil. The cheese clings to the enchiladas when the foil is removed instead of to the foil. Another option is to spray regular foil with cooking spray.

prep: 3 minutes   **cook:** 5 minutes

LAST MINUTE CHICKEN FAJITAS

Fajitas are a quick favorite that the whole family will love. Substitute beef or shrimp for the chicken, or add onions or mushrooms to vary the flavor.

Cooking spray

1   pound chicken breast tenders, cut into bite-sized pieces

1   tablespoon fajita seasoning

1   (16-ounce) package frozen bell pepper stir-fry
    (such as Bird's Eye)

8   (6-inch) flour tortillas

½   cup (2 ounces) reduced-fat shredded Cheddar cheese

Salsa (optional)

1. Place a large nonstick skillet coated with cooking spray over medium-high heat. Add chicken and seasoning; stir-fry 2 minutes. Add bell pepper stir-fry; stir-fry 2 minutes or until chicken is done.
2. Warm tortillas according to package directions. Spoon ½ cup chicken mixture down center of each tortilla; sprinkle each with 1 tablespoon cheese. Roll up. Top with salsa, if desired. Yield: 4 servings (serving size: 2 fajitas).

POINTS:
7

exchanges:
2½ Starch
3 Very Lean Meat
1 Lean Meat

per serving:
Calories 372
Carbohydrate 36.4g
Fat 8.9g (saturated 3.2g)
Fiber 3.7g
Protein 36.5g
Cholesterol 76mg
Sodium 617mg
Calcium 186mg
Iron 2.1mg

Shortcut

Quick Thaw: Thaw the stir-fry mixture in a colander under cold running water. Drain well.

OVEN-FRIED CHICKEN TENDERS

photo, page 123

With this easy recipe, you'll never be tempted by drive-thru chicken again! The crushed cheese crackers add crunch and flavor to this kid-friendly recipe. Serve with honey Dijon mustard for a tangy dipping sauce.

POINTS:
6

exchanges:
1 Starch
4 Very Lean Meat
1 Fat

per serving:
Calories 261
Carbohydrate 16.5g
Fat 7.6g (saturated 1.7g)
Fiber 0.7g
Protein 29.4g
Cholesterol 68mg
Sodium 364mg
Calcium 46mg
Iron 1.8mg

1   pound chicken breast tenders

½   cup low-fat buttermilk (1%)

1½ cups reduced-fat cheese crackers, crushed

(such as reduced-fat Cheese Nips)

¾   teaspoon Creole seasoning

¼   teaspoon salt

Cooking spray

1   tablespoon vegetable oil

1. Preheat oven to 450°.

2. Combine chicken and buttermilk in a shallow bowl. Place crackers, Creole seasoning, and salt in a heavy-duty zip-top plastic bag. Crush crackers with a rolling pin or heel of hand.

3. Drain chicken, discarding buttermilk. Add chicken to bag, close, and shake to coat well.

4. Coat a baking sheet with cooking spray. Pour oil in center of baking sheet; heat oil at 450° for 3 minutes. Remove pan from oven; reduce heat to 400°. Spread hot oil with a spatula over an area just large enough to accommodate chicken. Quickly place chicken in oil on pan. Bake at 400° for 10 minutes; turn, and bake an additional 3 minutes or until done. Yield: 4 servings (serving size: 3 chicken tenders).

Shortcut

Easy Clean Up: For easier clean up, use zip-top plastic bags to crush crackers and bread the chicken tenders.

prep: 7 minutes **cook:** 14 minutes

TENDER CHICKEN IN GRAVY

The classic look and taste of this recipe is so comforting that it should satisfy your pickiest eater. Serve over wild rice for a delicious hearty meal.

Cooking spray

1   pound chicken breast tenders

1   (14-ounce) can fat-free, less-sodium chicken broth

½   teaspoon dried thyme

¼   teaspoon garlic powder

¼   teaspoon salt

¼   teaspoon pepper

½   cup fat-free evaporated milk

2   tablespoons all-purpose flour

1   tablespoon light butter

2   tablespoons chopped fresh parsley, divided

LOW POINTS:
4

exchanges:
½ Starch
4 Very Lean Meat

per serving:
Calories 184
Carbohydrate 7.4g
Fat 3.0g (saturated 1.4g)
Fiber 0.3g
Protein 30.6g
Cholesterol 72mg
Sodium 537mg
Calcium 109mg
Iron 1.3mg

1. Place a large nonstick skillet coated with cooking spray over medium-high heat. Add chicken, and cook 2 minutes or until lightly browned. Turn chicken; add broth, thyme, garlic powder, salt, and pepper; bring to a boil. Cover, reduce heat, and simmer 3 minutes or until chicken is no longer pink in center. Remove chicken from pan; set aside and keep warm.

2. Whisk together milk and flour in a small bowl. Bring broth mixture to a boil. Cook 4 minutes or until liquid is reduced to 1 cup. Slowly stir in milk mixture, butter, and 1 tablespoon parsley. Cook, stirring constantly, until gravy thickens. Serve over chicken; sprinkle with remaining parsley. Yield: 4 servings (serving size: 3 chicken tenders and ¼ cup gravy).

Shortcut

No-Lump Gravy: Use a whisk rather than a fork or spoon to combine flour and milk. Stir constantly to keep the gravy from forming lumps as it cooks and thickens.

prep: 2 minutes   **cook:** 15 minutes   **stand:** 3 minutes

CREAMY CHICKEN AND BROCCOLI

This is a quick version of the popular 1970s casserole, Chicken Divan. If you like, sprinkle 2 tablespoons of toasted breadcrumbs on top before serving.

POINTS:
5

exchanges:
1 Starch
3 Very Lean Meat
1 Lean Meat

per serving:
Calories 251
Carbohydrate 13.3g
Fat 6.0g (saturated 3.1g)
Fiber 2.1g
Protein 35.3g
Cholesterol 83mg
Sodium 372mg
Calcium 189mg
Iron 1.3mg

1   (10-ounce) can 98%-fat-free cream of chicken soup
¼   cup fat-free sour cream
1   (10-ounce) package frozen broccoli spears
Cooking spray
1   pound chicken breast tenders
½   cup (2 ounces) reduced-fat shredded Cheddar cheese

1. Combine soup and sour cream in a small bowl.

2. Place frozen broccoli in a colander and run under cold water 30 to 45 seconds or until spears are separated and partially thawed; drain well on paper towels.

3. Heat a large nonstick skillet coated with cooking spray over medium-high heat. Place chicken and broccoli in pan. Spoon sour cream mixture over chicken and broccoli.

4. Heat until mixture comes to a boil. Cover, reduce heat to medium, and simmer 12 minutes or until chicken is done. Remove from heat; sprinkle evenly with cheese. Cover and let stand 3 minutes or until cheese melts. Yield: 4 servings (serving size: 1 cup).

Shortcut

Quick and Tender: Chicken tenders are perfect for this recipe because they cook quickly without getting tough.

Easy Sides

HERBED BREAD KNOTS

photo, page 82

These pretty breadsticks may look difficult, but they're simple to make using refrigerated breadstick dough. They are a delicious accompaniment to Italian Beef and Polenta Bake (page 79).

LOW POINTS:
3

exchanges:
2 Starch

per serving:
Calories 161
Carbohydrate 25.5g
Fat 3.6g (saturated 0.6g)
Fiber 0.7g
Protein 5.3g
Cholesterol 2mg
Sodium 445mg
Calcium 44mg
Iron 1.5mg

1   (11-ounce) can refrigerated soft breadstick dough

Butter-flavored cooking spray

¼   teaspoon Italian seasoning

⅛   teaspoon garlic powder

3   tablespoons grated Parmesan cheese

1. Preheat oven to 350°.

2. Separate breadsticks according to package directions. Loosely tie each breadstick in a knot; place on a baking sheet coated with cooking spray. Sprinkle evenly with Italian seasoning and garlic powder; top evenly with cheese. Bake at 350° for 15 minutes or until lightly browned. Yield: 6 servings (serving size: 2 bread knots).

Shortcut

Easy Homemade Bread Knots: Refrigerated breadstick dough cuts back dramatically on the time spent making these knots. The dough is very pliable and can easily be stretched and tied into a loose knot for an attractive presentation.

CHEESY CHILI BREADSTICKS

Present these cheesy breadsticks the same way your favorite pizza parlor would.
Leave them connected and allow your guests to tear off individual pieces.
Marinara sauce makes a delicious dipping sauce.

1   (11-ounce) can refrigerated soft breadstick dough

Butter-flavored cooking spray

½   teaspoon chili powder

½   cup (2 ounces) shredded Monterey Jack cheese with
     jalapeño peppers

1. Preheat oven to 375°.

2. Unroll breadstick dough; separate dough into 2 rectangles
(do not separate individual breadsticks). Place both pieces of
dough on an ungreased baking sheet. Coat dough with cooking
spray; sprinkle with chili powder.

3. Bake at 375° for 10 minutes. Sprinkle cheese evenly over
dough. Bake an additional 2 minutes or until cheese melts. Yield:
12 servings (serving size: 1 breadstick).

LOW **POINTS:**
2

exchange:
1 Starch

per serving:
Calories 92
Carbohydrate 12.8g
Fat 2.9g (saturated 1.0g)
Fiber 0.4g
Protein 3.2g
Cholesterol 5mg
Sodium 226mg
Calcium 34mg
Iron 0.7mg

Shortcut

Shredded Cheese: For convenience, many flavors and
blends of cheeses are available preshredded. Cold cheese
is easier to shred, especially if you use a hand grater.

GRAPEFRUIT-WALNUT GREEN SALAD

Serve this refreshing salad with Lemon Crusted Grouper (page 31) or
Chicken Pasta Primavera (page 67).

LOW **POINTS:**
1

exchanges:
1 Vegetable
½ Fruit
½ Fat

per serving:
Calories 74
Carbohydrate 10.3g
Fat 3.6g (saturated 0.4g)
Fiber 1.9g
Protein 1.9g
Cholesterol 0mg
Sodium 79mg
Calcium 32mg
Iron 1.0mg

1   (10-ounce) package hearts of romaine mix

1   cup refrigerated unsweetened red grapefruit sections

¼   cup grapefruit juice from jar of sections

2   teaspoons olive oil

1   tablespoon honey

⅛   teaspoon salt

⅛   teaspoon freshly ground black pepper

1   tablespoon chopped walnuts, toasted

1. Combine romaine and grapefruit sections; toss gently.

2. Combine grapefruit juice and next 4 ingredients in a small bowl; stir well with a whisk. Add dressing to salad mixture; toss to coat. Sprinkle with walnuts; toss once. Yield: 4 servings (serving size: 1½ cups).

Shortcut

Sweet Sectioned Fruit: When you're in a hurry to make a nutritious accompaniment to your meal, there's no time to section citrus fruit. Now you can purchase precut orange and grapefruit sections in the produce department. This fruit has no added syrup or sugar—it's packed in its own juice. You get the same calories and nutrients you would if you sectioned your own citrus fruit.

prep: 2 minutes   cook: 8 minutes

ROASTED ASPARAGUS

Enjoy this flavorful roasted asparagus as a side or on top of your favorite pasta or salad.
Try pairing it with Veal Chops with Portobello Sauce (page 97).

1¼ pound asparagus spears, rinsed and trimmed

1   tablespoon olive oil

¼   teaspoon salt

¼   teaspoon black pepper

Cooking spray

1. Preheat oven to 400°.

2. Toss asparagus with next 3 ingredients. Arrange asparagus in a single layer on a foil-lined baking sheet coated with cooking spray. Bake at 400° for 8 to 10 minutes or until tender, shaking pan often to roast asparagus evenly. Yield: 4 servings (serving size: about ¾ cup).

LOW POINTS:
1

exchanges:
2 Vegetable

per serving:
Calories 61
Carbohydrate 5.0g
Fat 3.4g (saturated 0.5g)
Fiber 2.5g
Protein 2.5g
Cholesterol 0mg
Sodium 147mg
Calcium 25mg
Iron 0.5mg

Shortcut

Rubber Bands Lend a Hand: Leave the rubber bands on the bunch of asparagus, and use a sharp knife to cut off the ends of the stalks about where the stalk begins to turn green. Remove bands, and then rinse well. Try this approach and you'll never go back to the traditional method of snapping off the tough ends.

GARLIC-ROASTED GREEN BEANS

Combine the fresh sweetness of crisp green beans and the essence of roasted garlic for a delicious side dish. Serve with Lemon Turkey Cutlets (page 72).

LOW POINTS:
1

exchanges:
2 Vegetable

per serving:
Calories 48
Carbohydrate 8.8g
Fat 1.3g (saturated 0.2g)
Fiber 3.9g
Protein 2.2g
Cholesterol 0mg
Sodium 8mg
Calcium 45mg
Iron 1.2mg

1   pound green beans

2   garlic cloves, sliced

Olive oil-flavored cooking spray

2   teaspoons lemon juice

1   teaspoon olive oil

1   teaspoon salt-free lemon pepper seasoning

1. Preheat oven to 450°.

2. Wash beans and trim ends. Place beans and garlic in a single layer on a foil-lined baking sheet. Coat beans and garlic with cooking spray; toss well. Drizzle lemon juice and olive oil over beans and garlic; sprinkle with lemon pepper seasoning.

3. Bake, uncovered, at 450° for 8 to 10 minutes or until beans are crisp-tender, stirring once. Yield: 4 servings (serving size: 1 cup).

Shortcut

Nice and Neat: If you're a meticulous individual, you'll like this shortcut. Rinse green beans in a colander under running water. Gather beans into small bunches with like ends together and cut off ends with a sharp knife. When you finish, you'll have a neat stack of green beans ready to cook.

prep: 2 minutes   **cook:** 9 minutes

ASIAN BROCCOLI STIR-FRY

Sweet-and-sour sauce enhances the fresh flavors in this Asian dish. Serve with
Curried Pork Chops (page 98) or Balsamic-Glazed Chicken (page 100).

2   teaspoons olive oil

Cooking spray

4   cups broccoli florets

1   (8-ounce) package presliced mushrooms

½   cup drained, sliced water chestnuts

3   tablespoons sweet-and-sour sauce (such as Lawry's
    Sesame Ginger)

2   tablespoons water

¼   teaspoon salt

1. Heat oil in a large nonstick skillet coated with cooking spray
over medium-high heat. Add broccoli and mushrooms; cook,
stirring occasionally, 7 minutes or until broccoli is crisp-tender.
Reduce heat to medium; add water chestnuts and remaining
ingredients. Stir-fry 1 minute or until thoroughly heated. Yield:
4 servings (serving size: ¾ cup).

LOW **POINTS:**
1

exchanges:
2 Vegetable
½ Fat

per serving:
Calories 85
Carbohydrate 14.1g
Fat 2.7g (saturated 0.4g)
Fiber 4.1g
Protein 3.9g
Cholesterol 0mg
Sodium 215mg
Calcium 41mg
Iron 9.6mg

Shortcut

No Chopping Required: It often takes longer to slice the
ingredients for a vegetable stir-fry than it does to cook
them. There's no chopping needed for this quick side dish.
Use bagged broccoli florets, fresh presliced mushrooms,
canned sliced water chestnuts, and a bottled sauce to
create a flavorful, simple stir-fry.

prep: 7 minutes   **cook:** 7 minutes

PESTO-TOSSED CAULIFLOWER

Turn steamed cauliflower into a special side dish by tossing the florets in pesto.

LOW **POINTS:**
1

exchanges:
1 Vegetable
1 Fat

per serving:
Calories 74
Carbohydrate 5.9g
Fat 4.7g (saturated 1.2g)
Fiber 2.8g
Protein 3.8g
Cholesterol 3mg
Sodium 252mg
Calcium 92mg
Iron 0.8mg

4   cups cauliflower florets

½   cup water

2½   tablespoons commercial pesto

¼   teaspoon salt

¼   teaspoon freshly ground black pepper

1. Place cauliflower in a microwave-safe bowl; pour water over cauliflower. Cover with plastic wrap; vent. Microwave at HIGH 6 minutes or until done.

2. Drain cauliflower, and return to dish. Add pesto, salt, and pepper; toss well. Cover; microwave at HIGH 1 minute or until hot. Yield: 4 servings (serving size: 1 cup).

Shortcut

Plenty of Pesto: Pesto has a very concentrated flavor, so a small amount goes a long way. That makes it ideal for shortcut cooking. Keep this ingredient in your refrigerator for last minute meals such as Grilled Pesto Salmon (page 57) or Chicken Pesto Pockets (page 70).

prep: 5 minutes   **cook:** 20 minutes

ROASTED ROSEMARY POTATOES
photo, page 64

Rosemary transforms packaged potato wedges into a tempting accompaniment to any dish. Serve with Pot Roast with Balsamic Onions (page 59) for a 6-**POINTS** meal.

1	tablespoon olive oil
1	teaspoon bottled minced garlic
1	(1-pound, 4-ounce) package new potato wedges
1	teaspoon dried rosemary
¾	teaspoon salt
½	teaspoon freshly ground black pepper

Cooking spray

1. Preheat oven to 450°.

2. Combine oil and garlic in a large bowl.

3. Add potatoes; toss to coat. Sprinkle potato mixture with rosemary, salt, and pepper; toss well.

4. Place potatoes in a single layer on a foil-lined baking sheet coated with cooking spray. Bake at 450° for 15 minutes. Turn potatoes with a spatula. Bake an additional 5 minutes or until browned and crisp. Yield: 4 servings (serving size: 1 cup).

LOW **POINTS:**
2

exchanges:
1 Starch
1 Fat

per serving:
Calories 120
Carbohydrate 18.1g
Fat 3.4g (saturated 0.5g)
Fiber 3.7g
Protein 3.6g
Cholesterol 0mg
Sodium 589mg
Calcium 6mg
Iron 0.8mg

Shortcut

Precut Potatoes: The original recipe used 1½ pounds of red potatoes, quartered. We substituted precut new potato wedges available in the refrigerated produce or dairy sections of the supermarket.

CHEDDAR MASHED POTATOES

Garlic and herb cheese spread and Cheddar cheese double the flavor of this familiar side dish.

LOW POINTS:
3

exchanges:
1½ Starch
1 Fat

per serving:
Calories 158
Carbohydrate 21.4g
Fat 5.1g (saturated 2.7g)
Fiber 1.8g
Protein 6.8g
Cholesterol 17mg
Sodium 585mg
Calcium 159mg
Iron 0.4mg

1   (22-ounce) package frozen mashed potatoes

1⅓ cups 1% low-fat milk

⅓   cup spreadable cheese with garlic and herbs
    (such as Alouette)

¼   cup (1 ounce) reduced-fat shredded sharp Cheddar cheese

¼   teaspoon salt

⅛   teaspoon pepper

1. Prepare mashed potatoes according to package directions, using 1% low-fat milk. Stir in remaining ingredients. Yield: 5 servings (serving size: ½ cup).

Shortcut

Spreads for Any Occasion: Vary the flavor of cheese spread and you have a new recipe. Other cheese spread flavors include Sundried Tomato and Basil, Vegetable Garden, and Lite Herbs.

prep: 2 minutes   **cook:** 4 minutes

CRUSTY BROILED TOMATOES

These broiled tomatoes get an unexpected twist from the creamy mustard Dijonnaise,
a surprisingly 0-**POINT** ingredient.

2   large tomatoes

1   tablespoon creamy mustard blend (such as Dijonnaise)

¼   cup Italian-seasoned breadcrumbs

¼   cup (1 ounce) preshredded fresh Parmesan cheese

⅛   teaspoon salt

⅛   teaspoon ground black pepper

⅛   teaspoon ground red pepper

Cooking spray

1. Preheat broiler.

2. Cut tomatoes in half crosswise. Drain halves on a layer of
paper towels, cut sides down.

3. Spread creamy mustard blend evenly over cut sides of tomato
halves.

4. Combine breadcrumbs and next 4 ingredients in a small bowl.
Spoon breadcrumb mixture evenly over tomato halves. Coat with
cooking spray. Place tomato halves on a foil-lined baking sheet.
Broil, on middle oven rack, 4 minutes or until tomatoes are hot
and lightly browned. Yield: 4 servings (serving size: ½ tomato).

LOW **POINTS:**
1

exchanges:
½ Starch
1 Vegetable

per serving:
Calories 71
Carbohydrate 10.5g
Fat 1.9g (saturated 1.0g)
Fiber 1.4g
Protein 3.8g
Cholesterol 4mg
Sodium 418mg
Calcium 75mg
Iron 0.7mg

Shortcut

No Hassle Crumbs: Keep seasoned breadcrumbs on hand
for a quick hassle-free side dish.

SUMMER SQUASH SAUTÉ

Add this healthy, quick side to any main dish such as Moroccan Roasted Salmon (page 90) or Sweet Spiced Barbecue Chicken (page 141) for a burst of color and extra nutrients.

LOW POINTS:
1

exchanges:
1½ Vegetable
½ Fat

per serving:
Calories 76
Carbohydrate 7.6g
Fat 3.9g (saturated 1.2g)
Fiber 2.8g
Protein 3.5g
Cholesterol 4mg
Sodium 677mg
Calcium 93mg
Iron 0.8mg

2   teaspoons olive oil

1   zucchini, thinly sliced

1   yellow squash, thinly sliced

3   garlic cloves, thinly sliced

½   teaspoon salt

½   teaspoon freshly ground black pepper

1   cup diced seeded tomato (about 1 large)

¼   cup (1 ounce) preshredded fresh Parmesan cheese

1. Heat oil in a large nonstick skillet over medium heat. Add zucchini and next 4 ingredients; sauté 5 minutes. Add tomato; sauté 2 minutes or until vegetables are tender. Sprinkle with cheese. Serve immediately. Yield: 4 servings (serving size: ¾ cup).

Shortcut

Speedy Seeding: To seed tomatoes quickly, cut the tomato in half crosswise. Squeeze each half lightly and the seeds will slip out, or use your finger or a small spoon to remove the seeds.

Sweets
and
Treats

MIXED BERRIES WITH RASPBERRY CREAM SAUCE

photo, opposite page

Try this easy, creamy raspberry sauce over any variety of fresh berries, or try it as a topping for ice cream or angel food cake.

LOW POINTS:
2

exchanges:
2 Fruit

per serving:
Calories 131
Carbohydrate 30.2g
Fat 0.6g (saturated 0.0g)
Fiber 5.0g
Protein 2.3g
Cholesterol 0mg
Sodium 37mg
Calcium 59mg
Iron 0.6mg

¼ cup fat-free sour cream

2 tablespoons raspberry preserves

2 tablespoons fat-free half-and-half

3 cups mixed berries (such as raspberries, blueberries, or strawberries)

1. Combine sour cream, preserves, and half-and-half in a small bowl; stir with a wire whisk to combine. Divide berries evenly among serving bowls; spoon sauce evenly over berries. Yield: 3 servings (serving size: 1 cup berries and 2 tablespoons sauce).

Shortcut

Fresh Fruit Options: Substitute any combination of cut fresh fruit for the berries in this recipe. Most supermarkets have fresh fruit combos in plastic containers in the produce section.

Mixed Berries with Raspberry Cream Sauce,
opposite page

Chocolate Toffee Mousse,
page 170

Chewy Chocolate-
Peanut Butter Bars,
page 174

RICE PUDDING-TROPICAL FRUIT PARFAIT

Dried fruits such as pineapple, passion fruit, and papaya add a fun tropical
flavor to everyday rice pudding.

LOW POINTS:
3

exchanges:
1 Starch
1½ Fruit

per serving:
Calories 182
Carbohydrate 38.6g
Fat 2.8g (saturated 2.0g)
Fiber 2.8g
Protein 3.5g
Cholesterol 5mg
Sodium 96mg
Calcium 89mg
Iron 1.2mg

¼   cup low-fat commercial rice pudding

¼   cup dried tropical mixed fruit (such as Del Monte Sun Fresh)

2   teaspoons flaked sweetened coconut

1. Spoon rice pudding into a stemmed glass; top with fruit and
sprinkle with coconut. Yield: 1 serving (serving size: ½ cup).

Shortcut

Easy As 1-2-3: This simple treat can be made quickly by
using three convenient grocery store items: refrigerated rice
pudding, dried fruit, and flaked coconut. If you have time,
toast the coconut to enhance its natural flavors.

prep: 2 minutes

RASPBERRY CARAMEL SUNDAE

Get creative when making this simple but classic sundae by experimenting
with different fruit and sauce combinations.

½ cup vanilla low-fat ice cream

¼ cup fresh raspberries

1 tablespoon fat-free caramel sundae syrup (such as Smucker's)

1. Place ice cream in a stemmed glass; sprinkle with raspberries
and drizzle with caramel syrup. Yield: 1 serving.

Shortcut

Caramel Is Key: Caramel sundae syrup is a quick on-hand
topping when you need something sweet. Not only is it
delicious over ice cream, it can add a burst of flavor to
pound cake, fresh fruit, or frozen yogurt.

LOW **POINTS:**
3

exchanges:
2 Starch
½ Fruit

per serving:
Calories 170
Carbohydrate 34.1g
Fat 2.2g (saturated 1.0g)
Fiber 3.1g
Protein 3.8g
Cholesterol 5mg
Sodium 105mg
Calcium 117mg
Iron 0.2mg

QUADRUPLE CHOCOLATE SUNDAE

photo, page 63

This dessert looks so elegant but is a snap to make. Serve it after a special dinner, and you are sure to bring a smile to your guests' faces.

POINTS:
4

exchanges:
3 Starch

per serving:
Calories 230
Carbohydrate 41.2g
Fat 4.3g (saturated 1.7g)
Fiber 3.2g
Protein 4.7g
Cholesterol 7mg
Sodium 130mg
Calcium 135mg
Iron 1.2mg

½ cup chocolate low-fat ice cream

1 tablespoon fat-free chocolate sundae syrup
(such as Hershey's)

1 teaspoon chocolate sprinkles

1 chocolate wafer cookie

1. Spoon ice cream into a small bowl; drizzle with chocolate syrup and top with chocolate sprinkles. Press chocolate wafer partially into ice cream. Yield: 1 serving.

Shortcut

Tiny Scoop Teaser: Use a melon baller to make smaller ice cream scoops. Multiple scoops tease your mind into thinking you are eating more than you actually are.

prep: 13 minutes

BLACK FOREST TRIFLE
photo, page 4

Keep angel food cake, cherry pie filling, pudding cups, and frozen whipped topping on hand for a quick dessert.

1 (16-ounce) angel food cake, cubed

1 (20-ounce) can no-sugar-added cherry pie filling

4 (3.5-ounce) cups fat-free chocolate pudding (such as Jello Snack Pack)

1 (8-ounce) carton frozen fat-free whipped topping, thawed

¼ cup chocolate curls

1. Place half of cake cubes in a 2-quart trifle bowl; spoon half of cherry pie filling over cake. Spread 2 pudding cups over cherry pie filling, and top with half of whipped topping. Repeat layers. Top with chocolate curls. Chill, if desired. Yield: 12 servings (serving size: 1 cup).

POINTS:
4

exchanges:
2½ Starch

per serving:
Calories 190
Carbohydrate 40.6g
Fat 1.2g (saturated 0.6g)
Fiber 1.5g
Protein 3.2g
Cholesterol 1mg
Sodium 352mg
Calcium 84mg
Iron 0.4mg

Shortcut

No Trifle Bowl: You don't need a special trifle bowl to make this recipe. Any 2-quart bowl will work.

CHOCOLATE TOFFEE MOUSSE

photo, page 158

Crunchy toffee bits, chocolate cookie crumbs, and smooth, creamy mousse make it hard to say no to this decadent dessert.

POINTS:
6

exchanges:
3 Starch
1 Fat

per serving:
Calories 297
Carbohydrate 49.8g
Fat 7.7g (saturated 4.0g)
Fiber 1.2g
Protein 4.9g
Cholesterol 10mg
Sodium 391mg
Calcium 184mg
Iron 0.8mg

¾ cup teddy bear-shaped chocolate graham cracker cookies, crushed (such as Chocolate Teddy Grahams)

2½ cups 1% chocolate low-fat milk

1 (2.1-ounce) package sugar-free chocolate instant pudding mix

1 (8-ounce) carton frozen reduced-calorie whipped topping, thawed and divided

2 (1.4-ounce) chocolate toffee bars, crushed and divided (such as Skor)

1. Divide chocolate crumbs evenly among 6 parfait glasses.

2. Pour milk into a large bowl; add pudding mix and whisk until thick. Fold in 1½ cups whipped topping and ¼ cup crushed toffee bar. Spoon pudding mixture evenly over crumbs in parfait glasses.

3. Top with remaining whipped topping and crushed toffee bar. Chill until ready to serve. Yield: 6 servings.

Shortcut

Quick Crush: Place cookies and toffee bars in separate heavy-duty zip-top bags. Crush with a rolling pin.

prep: 12 minutes   **cook:** 2 minutes

CHOCOLATE-DRIZZLED FRUIT TARTS

Use the season's fresh fruit to dress these dainty tarts. We liked strawberries, raspberries, and kiwi slices.

1	(8-ounce) tub light cream cheese
⅓	cup powdered sugar
1	teaspoon grated orange rind
1	tablespoon fresh orange juice
1	(4-ounce) package miniature graham cracker piecrusts
2	cups assorted fresh fruit, sliced
1	ounce semisweet chocolate, melted

1. Stir together first 4 ingredients in a small bowl. Spoon into piecrusts. Arrange fruit on top of cream cheese mixture. Drizzle with chocolate. Yield: 6 servings (serving size: 1 tart).

POINTS:
5

exchanges:
1 Starch
1 Fruit
1½ Fat

per serving:
Calories 224
Carbohydrate 29.0g
Fat 10.0g (saturated 3.7g)
Fiber 2.6g
Protein 5.5g
Cholesterol 13mg
Sodium 264mg
Calcium 40mg
Iron 0.7mg

Shortcut

Drizzle Ease: After melting chocolate in the microwave, use the tines of a fork to easily drizzle the melted chocolate over the tarts.

CHOCOLATE DATE BALLS

For only 1-**POINT** each, these treats are the perfect snack to satisfy a chocolate craving.
They are also delicious rolled in cocoa, coconut, or powdered sugar. Store them in an airtight
container for up to a week in the refrigerator.

LOW POINTS:
1

exchange:
½ Starch

per serving:
Calories 41
Carbohydrate 5.5g
Fat 2.0g (saturated 0.2g)
Fiber 0.5g
Protein 0.8g
Cholesterol 0mg
Sodium 21mg
Calcium 16mg
Iron 0.1mg

1   tablespoon instant nonfat dry milk

1   tablespoon plus 1 teaspoon fat-free milk

1   teaspoon vanilla extract

⅔   cup chocolate graham cracker crumbs (about 4 crackers)

4   pitted dates, chopped

2   tablespoons finely chopped pecans

1. Combine first 3 ingredients in a small bowl. Stir in graham
cracker crumbs. Stir in dates.

2. Shape crumb mixture into 6 (1 to 1¼-inch) balls.

3. Roll balls in pecans. Cover and chill 2 hours. Yield: 6 balls
(serving size: 1 ball).

Shortcut

Just Enough: Most recipes for chocolate truffles or date
balls yield several dozen. We've cut the yield back on this
recipe so that you can enjoy the treats without spending a
lot of time making them.

prep: 6 minutes **cook:** 24 minutes

FUDGY TURTLE BROWNIES

These rich, ooey-gooey brownies are irresistible, and only 3-**POINTS** each! Pair with a glass of fat-free milk for a too-good-to-be-true snack or dessert.

1   (20.5-ounce) package low-fat fudge brownie mix
    (such as Betty Crocker Sweet Rewards)

Cooking spray

½   cup fat-free caramel apple dip

¼   cup chopped pecans

¼   cup semisweet chocolate minichips

1. Preheat oven to 350°.

2. Prepare brownie batter according to package directions. Pour into a 13 x 9-inch pan lined with foil and coated with cooking spray. Bake at 350° for 24 minutes.

3. Spoon caramel dip into a small zip-top plastic bag; snip a tiny hole in one corner of bag. Drizzle caramel sauce over warm brownies; sprinkle with pecans and chocolate minichips. Cool on a wire rack. Yield: 24 servings (serving size: 1 brownie).

LOW **POINTS:**
3

exchanges:
2 Starch

per serving:
Calories 136
Carbohydrate 26.3g
Fat 3.3g (saturated 1.1g)
Fiber 0.9g
Protein 1.8g
Cholesterol 0mg
Sodium 107mg
Calcium 4mg
Iron 0.9mg

Shortcut

Line It Up: Line baking pan with foil allowing allowing foil to extend over edge of pan. This method will prevent brownies from sticking. After brownies have cooled, lift the sheet of foil out of the pan and place on a flat surface. Brownies will be easier to cut and serve.

CHEWY CHOCOLATE-PEANUT BUTTER BARS

photo, page 159

To get the maximum amount of creaminess for the same number of **POINTS**,
use regular extra-chunky peanut butter instead of reduced-fat.

LOW POINTS:
3

exchanges:
1½ Starch
1 Fat

per serving:
Calories 146
Carbohydrate 19.1g
Fat 6.8g (saturated 2.3g)
Fiber 1.1g
Protein 4.1g
Cholesterol 1mg
Sodium 63mg
Calcium 62mg
Iron 0.4mg

⅔ cup extra-chunky peanut butter

1 (14-ounce) can fat-free sweetened condensed milk, divided

1 teaspoon vanilla extract, divided

1 cup semisweet chocolate chips

1. Line an 8-inch square baking pan with foil.

2. Place peanut butter and ⅔ cup sweetened condensed milk in
a medium bowl. Microwave at HIGH 2½ minutes. Stir and
microwave 30 seconds. Stir in ½ teaspoon vanilla. Spread mixture
in pan, pressing into an even layer with fingers.

3. Place remaining sweetened condensed milk and chocolate
chips in a medium bowl. Microwave at HIGH 1½ minutes. Add
remaining vanilla; stir until smooth. Pour chocolate mixture over
peanut butter mixture; spread with a small spatula. Chill until
firm. Cut into 20 rectangular pieces. Store in an airtight container
in refrigerator. Yield: 20 servings (serving size: 1 piece).

Shortcut

Secret Tools: Foil and a pizza cutter are the two secret
tools that make this recipe mess-free. Lining the pan with
foil makes clean up a snap. Use a pizza cutter for a quick,
precise slice.

WARM CINNAMON SWIRLS
photo, page 84

The aroma of these 1-**POINT** treats when baking is sure to lure anyone out of bed. Serve with a mug of hot flavored coffee or a glass of cold fat-free milk.

1   (8-ounce) package reduced-fat crescent rolls

4   teaspoons bottled cinnamon-sugar

Cooking spray

½   cup powdered sugar

2   teaspoons 1% low-fat milk

LOW POINTS:
1

exchange:
1 Starch

per serving:
Calories 55
Carbohydrate 8.5g
Fat 1.8g (saturated 0.4g)
Fiber 0.1g
Protein 0.8g
Cholesterol 0mg
Sodium 94mg
Calcium 3mg
Iron 0.4mg

1. Preheat oven to 375°.

2. Unroll crescent roll dough onto work surface. Separate dough crosswise with a sharp knife. Press perforations together with fingers. Sprinkle each portion of dough with 2 teaspoons cinnamon-sugar. Roll up 1 portion of dough, starting at long side and pressing firmly to eliminate air pockets; pinch seam to seal. Cut roll into 10 slices. Place rolls, cut sides down, on a baking sheet coated with cooking spray. Repeat with remaining dough and cinnamon-sugar.

3. Bake at 375° for 10 to 12 minutes or until golden.

4. Whisk together powdered sugar and milk until smooth; drizzle over warm rolls with a small whisk. Yield: 20 swirls (serving size: 1 swirl).

Shortcut

Make Ahead Swirls: Freeze unglazed swirls in an airtight container for up to a month. When ready to eat, defrost in the microwave and drizzle with fresh glaze.

Beverages
and
Snacks

prep: 1 minute   **cook:** 3 minutes

MOCCACHINO

Chocolate soy milk is the secret to making this warm drink rich and creamy.
If you prefer, you can substitute low-fat chocolate milk for the soy milk.

⅔   cup strong brewed coffee

⅓   cup chocolate soy milk (such as Silk)

1   tablespoon frozen reduced–calorie whipped topping, thawed

Fat-free hot cocoa mix (optional)

1. Combine coffee and milk; pour into a mug. Microwave at HIGH 2 minutes or until hot. Spoon whipped topping onto coffee mixture. Sprinkle with cocoa mix, if desired. Serve immediately. Yield: 1 serving (serving size: 1 cup).

Shortcut

Instant Coffee: Quickly make a cup of coffee using instant coffee granules. Stir 1½ teaspoons instant coffee granules into ⅔ cup boiling water.

LOW **POINTS:**
1

exchange:
1 Starch

per serving:
Calories 63
Carbohydrate 9.2g
Fat 1.8g (saturated 0.7g)
Fiber 0.0g
Protein 2.1g
Cholesterol 0mg
Sodium 38mg
Calcium 23mg
Iron 0.7mg

RASPBERRY TEA

Substitute your favorite flavored syrup for the raspberry syrup used in this recipe.
For a 0-**POINT** drink, use sugar-free flavored syrup.

LOW POINTS:
2

4   cups unsweetened brewed tea

½   cup raspberry-flavored syrup

Lime wedges (optional)

exchange:
1 Starch

1. Combine tea and syrup in a pitcher. Serve over ice; garnish with lime wedges, if desired. Yield: 4 servings (serving size: 1 cup).

per serving:
Calories 106
Carbohydrate 26.6g
Fat 0.0g (saturated 0.0g)
Fiber 0.0g
Protein 0.0g
Cholesterol 0mg
Sodium 8mg
Calcium 6mg
Iron 0.8mg

Shortcut

Practical Purchases: Purchase unsweetened tea from the grocery store instead of brewing your own. You can also purchase other flavored syrups such as blackberry, strawberry, peach, or orange from your local grocery store or coffee shop.

SPARKLING FRUIT JUICE COOLER

If you don't have cran-cherry juice on hand, substitute any cran-fruit drink.

½ cup cranberry-cherry juice drink

¼ cup orange juice

¼ cup diet lemon-lime soda (such as diet Sprite)

1 lime wedge

1. Combine first 3 ingredients in an ice-filled glass; stir. Squeeze lime into drink, and add wedge to glass. Yield: 1 serving (serving size: 1 cup).

Shortcut

Don't Go Flat: Canned or bottled soft drinks lose their carbonation if left open. Use a bottle with a twist top to prevent the soda from going flat too quickly. Extra soda should be used within a week of opening.

LOW **POINTS:**
2

exchanges:
2 Fruit

per serving:
Calories 110
Carbohydrate 27.6g
Fat 0.0g (saturated 0.0g)
Fiber 0.3g
Protein 0.7g
Cholesterol 0mg
Sodium 8mg
Calcium 14mg
Iron 0.2mg

prep: 2 minutes

TANGY FRUIT COCKTAIL

Refresh with this blend of cranberry, apple, grapefruit, and lime juices.

LOW POINTS:
2

exchanges:
2 Fruit

per serving:
Calories 102
Carbohydrate 25.1g
Fat 0.2g (saturated 0.0g)
Fiber 0.2g
Protein 0.7g
Cholesterol 0mg
Sodium 6mg
Calcium 20mg
Iron 0.4mg

1½ cups reduced-calorie cranberry juice cocktail, chilled

1 cup apple juice, chilled

2 (6-ounce) cans pink grapefruit juice, chilled

¼ cup fresh lime juice (about 3 limes)

2 tablespoons granulated sugar substitute (such as Equal)

Lime slices (optional)

1. Combine first 5 ingredients in a pitcher; stir well. Serve juice over crushed ice. Garnish with lime slices, if desired. Yield: 4 servings (serving size: 1 cup).

Shortcut

Juicier Citrus: You'll get the most juice out of your limes by microwaving them at HIGH for 30 seconds and rolling them on a flat surface before slicing.

SPARKLING PEACH SLUSH

photo, page 160

Make this ahead of time into flavored ice cubes (as directed in step 1) then pull out as needed for a luncheon, Sunday brunch, or when ever you want a refreshing peach drink.

3   cups peach nectar

2   cups champagne

1. Pour 1½ cups peach nectar into each of 2 ice cube trays. Freeze at least 4 hours.

2. Place peach ice cubes and ¼ cup champagne in blender; process until smooth. Pour into a large pitcher; stir in remaining champagne. Yield: 4 servings (serving size: 1 cup).

Nonalcoholic Variation: Freeze peach nectar in ice cube trays. Process peach ice cubes with ¼ cup sparkling grape juice. Pour into pitcher, and stir in ¾ cup sparkling grape juice and 1 cup sparkling mineral water. Yield: 4 servings (serving size: 1 cup).

LOW **POINTS:**

2

exchanges:
½ Starch
½ Fruit

per serving:
Calories 89
Carbohydrate 3.3g
Fat 0.0g (saturated 0.0g)
Fiber 0.1g
Protein 0.3g
Cholesterol 0mg
Sodium 10mg
Calcium 10mg
Iron 0.5mg

Shortcut

Plan Ahead: Freeze peach nectar in ice cube trays, remove from trays, and store in zip-top plastic freezer bags.

FRUIT SMOOTHIE

Packed with disease-fighting nutrients and rich in fiber, this thick, fruity smoothie is the perfect pick-me-up first thing in the morning or in the middle of the day.

LOW POINTS:
3

exchanges:
3 Fruit

per serving:
Calories 170
Carbohydrate 43.7g
Fat 0.6g (saturated 0.2g)
Fiber 4.4g
Protein 1.4g
Cholesterol 0mg
Sodium 6mg
Calcium 25mg
Iron 0.8mg

⅓ cup coarsely chopped mango

¼ cup halved strawberries (about 3)

½ ripe banana, frozen

⅓ cup papaya nectar

2 tablespoons powdered sugar

1 cup ice cubes

1. Combine all ingredients in a blender; process until smooth.

Yield: 1 serving (serving size: 1 cup).

Shortcut

Go Bananas: Buy bananas when they are at a good price, and then freeze. To freeze, peel bananas, cut in half or quarter, place in a heavy duty zip-top plastic bag, and freeze. Keep frozen bananas on hand for recipes such as this smoothie. Frozen bananas can be stored up to 1 month.

RANCH POPCORN

Enjoy a new twist on everyday microwave popcorn. Tangy ranch dressing
enhances the flavor of this buttery, salty snack.

1   (3-ounce) package 94%-fat-free microwave popcorn

1   tablespoon light butter, melted

2¼ teaspoons dry ranch dressing mix

1. Microwave popcorn according to package directions. Place
popcorn in a large bowl.

2. Drizzle butter over popcorn. Sprinkle with dressing mix; toss
well. Yield: about 4 servings (serving size: 3 cups).

Shortcut

Toss It Up: Combine popcorn, butter, and dressing mix in a
gallon-sized zip-top plastic bag. Toss well. Store in zip-top
bag until ready to eat.

LOW **POINTS:**

1

exchange:

1 Starch

per serving:

Calories 78

Carbohydrate 15.3g

Fat 2.6g (saturated 1.0g)

Fiber 3.4g

Protein 2.5g

Cholesterol 5mg

Sodium 396mg

Calcium 0mg

Iron 0.4mg

prep: 2 minutes **cook:** 15 minutes

SAUSAGE AND SPINACH CHEESE DIP

For a hearty appetizer at your next party, serve this cheesy dip with baked tortilla chips.

LOW **POINTS:**

2

exchanges:
1½ Medium-Fat Meat

per serving:
Calories 115
Carbohydrate 6.1g
Fat 4.4g (saturated 2.7g)
Fiber 0.9g
Protein 11.2g
Cholesterol 26mg
Sodium 791mg
Calcium 229mg
Iron 0.8mg

1   (10-ounce) package frozen chopped spinach

1   (10.5-ounce) package 97%-fat-free sausage

1   (16-ounce) block light processed cheese, sliced (such as Velveeta Light)

1   (10-ounce) can diced tomatoes and green chiles, undrained

1. Thaw spinach in microwave according to package directions; drain well and squeeze dry.

2. Cook sausage in a nonstick skillet over medium-high heat until browned, stirring to crumble. Drain.

3. Combine cheese and tomatoes in a 2-quart microwave-safe bowl. Microwave, uncovered, at HIGH 5 minutes or until cheese melts, stirring after 2 minutes.

4. Add sausage and spinach to cheese mixture; stir well. Microwave at HIGH 2 minutes or until thoroughly heated. Serve with baked tortilla chips. Yield: 13 servings (serving size: ⅓ cup).

Shortcut

Quick Sausage Draining Tip: Very lean sausage often requires little draining because of its low fat content. Soak up any excess liquid in the pan with a few paper towels.

General Recipe Index

VEGETABLE COOKING CHART

Vegetable	Servings	Preparations	Cooking Instructions
Asparagus	3 to 4 per pound	Snap off tough ends. Remove scales, if desired.	To steam: Cook, covered, on a rack above boiling water 8 to 12 minutes. To boil: Cook, covered, in a small amount of boiling water 6 to 8 minutes or until crisp-tender.
Broccoli	3 to 4 per pound	Remove outer leaves and tough ends of lower stalks. Wash; cut into spears.	To steam: Cook, covered, on a rack above boiling water 15 to 18 minutes.
Carrots	4 per pound	Scrape; remove ends, and rinse. Leave tiny carrots whole; slice large carrots, or cut into strips.	Cook, covered, in a small amount of boiling water 8 to 10 minutes (slices) or 12 to 15 minutes (strips).
Cauliflower	4 per medium head	Remove outer leaves and stalk. Wash. Leave whole, or break into florets.	Cook, covered, in a small amount of boiling water 10 to 12 minutes (whole) or 8 to 10 minutes (florets).
Corn	4 per 4 large ears	Remove husks and silks. Leave corn on the cob, or cut off tips of kernels, and scrape cob with dull edge of knife.	Cook, covered, in boiling water to cover 10 minutes (on cob) or in a small amount of boiling water 8 to 10 minutes (cut).
Green beans	4 per pound	Wash; trim ends, and remove strings. Cut into 1½-inch pieces.	Cook, covered, in a small amount of boiling water 12 to 15 minutes.
Potatoes	3 to 4 per pound	Scrub; peel, if desired. Leave whole, slice, or cut into chunks.	To cook: Cook, covered, in a small amount of boiling water 30 to 40 minutes (whole) or 15 to 20 minutes (slices or chunks). To bake: Bake at 400° for 1 hour or until done.
Snow peas	4 per pound	Wash; trim ends, and remove tough strings.	Cook, covered, in a small amount of boiling water 3 to 5 minutes. Or cook over high heat in reduced-calorie margarine or in pan coated with cooking spray 3 to 5 minutes, stirring constantly.
Squash, summer	3 to 4 per pound	Wash; trim ends. Leave whole, slice, or chop.	To steam: Cook, covered, on a rack over boiling water 10 to 12 minutes (sliced or chopped). To boil: Cook, covered, in a small amount of boiling water 8 to 10 minutes (slices) or 15 minutes (whole).
Squash, winter *(including acorn, butternut, hubbard, and spaghetti)*	2 per pound	Rinse; cut in half, and remove all seeds.	To boil: Cook, covered, in boiling water 20 to 25 minutes. To bake: Place cut side down in shallow baking dish; add ½ inch water. Bake, uncovered, at 375° for 30 minutes. Turn and season, or fill; bake 20 to 30 minutes or until tender.